The School Library Resource Centre

Margaret Allan

Crosby Lockwood Staples   London

Granada Publishing Limited
First published 1974 by Crosby Lockwood Staples
Frogmore St Albans Herts
and 3 Upper James Street London W1R 4BP

ISBN 0 258 96933 4

Text set in 12 pt. Photon Times, printed by photolithography,
and bound in Great Britain at The Pitman Press, Bath

The School Library Resource Centre

Foreword

In surveying the literature of librarianship one is sometimes tempted to conclude that librarians should exercise constraint before they add to the information explosion, and yet there seems to be a very real shortage of works based on experience concerning the practice of librarianship to assist librarians in the more practical aspects of their professional careers – the operation and organization of library services.

Margaret Allan's recent retirement from a lifetime in libraries serving education was a serious loss to progressive librarianship. Her interest in librarianship can be appreciated from her willingness to be persuaded to set down her thoughts in the work which follows while recollection of the perennial battles and problems (which every librarian by definition has to face) are still freshly remembered. The work is pre-eminently based on a practical approach to library problems, deliberately tackling the points of detail which more theoretical approaches tend to overlook, and presented in a pleasantly fresh and direct style which is characteristic of Margaret Allan's work and of her contribution to librarianship.

There can be few sectors of librarianship where guidance is more needed than the school library, subject to persistent upheavals in educational restructuring, a rapidly changing pattern of educational methods and, in particular, an increasing emphasis on new media materials in conjunction with print. Effective library services in this field could have an enormous influence on library policy both in institutions serving higher education and in public library support for informal or continuous education. The efficient organization of resources at the school level as outlined in Margaret Allan's work is a prerequisite for registering that influence.

Her sometimes provocative remarks often have, I feel, a relevance to a much wider area of librarianship. Gone are the days (if they ever existed) when librarianship was a quiet secluded job ideal for the quiet, the shy, and those who couldn't find something better to do, for libraries are no longer merely associated with education, but are, as this book shows, an integral part of the education process itself.

B. J. Enright
University Librarian
University of Newcastle upon Tyne

Contents

FOR
MY STAFF
IN THE LIBRARY
OF
STOCKWELL COLLEGE OF EDUCATION
1963–1972

Acknowledgments

If progress is to be made, the sharing of experiences is essential among those involved, or likely to become involved, in the development from the traditional book library in education to the multi-media library.

The writing of this book has been made possible because of the nature of my professional involvement in education and the willingness of so many teachers to discuss with me problems of communication within the framework of education at different levels. Enumeration would be impossible and selection invidious, but to those concerned who now read this book I gratefully acknowledge my indebtedness, as I do simultaneously to their colleagues.

During the writing of this book, when I found myself with considerably less access to books and materials than I had been accustomed to for many years, I have received from a number of professional colleagues assistance which I greatly appreciated and now acknowledge with pleasure:

F. Hallworth, Director, Library and Museum Services, Wiltshire, who allowed me to include Plates 2 and 3 and Colour Plates 1 and 4; Ken Wood, Assistant Director;

Valeria Fea, Librarian, Services to Education and Young People, Wiltshire; Judith Atkinson, Area Librarian, Nailsea and Pam Hayden, School Library Centre, Somerset County Library; Peter King.

I should like to express my thanks also to the following who took such pains to provide me with photographs of equipment and samples of stationery for reproduction in the book to help those readers who might not be familiar with them:

Art Metal for Plate 6 and Colour Plates 2 and 3; Diana Wyllie Ltd for Plates 14 and 15; Don Gresswell Ltd for Plates 1, 4, 5, 7, 8, 9, 12, 13, 16 and 17 and Figures 1, 2, 3 and 4; Frank Wilson (Filing) Ltd for Plate 11 and Figure 25; Stor Cabinets Ltd for Plate 10.

The extracts on pages 13 and 18 are reprinted from *The school library: a force for education excellence* (1969) by Ruth Ann Davies by permission of R. R. Bowker Company (a Xerox Education Company), 1180 Avenue of the Americas, New York, New York 10036.

Among those interested and involved in the promotion of multi-media libraries I have enjoyed and greatly appreciated the shared understanding of Brian Enright and Tony Trebble. Their persuasive encouragement made me start this book but neither is in any way responsible for shortcomings which its readers may discern.

M.A.W.A.

CHAPTER ONE

Introduction

The evolution of education since the Education Act of 1944, together with what has become known as the information explosion, has called in question the role of the teacher. Although in the past decade industry and commerce have made considerable use of modern technological means of communication, the educational world appears to be lacking in its willingness to adapt its traditional teaching methods in order to make use of these new media. Consequently, although the younger generation accepts and uses modern media as part of its daily living, there are too many of the older generation in the educational field who still see these new means of communication as methods which the good teacher should not need to employ. Undoubtedly considerable contributions are being made, by a minority of individuals and groups, to the development of an understanding of the learning processes of children and students; but one is forced to ask where are all those good teachers whose capabilities enable them to be self-sufficient.

The days have gone when a lad served his apprenticeship in a trade which, with few changes, lasted his lifetime. The teacher found his place in that comparatively static situation and to a great extent was, over a long period of time, the fountain of knowledge for his pupils. The advent first of radio and later of television played a large part in changing this situation, bringing the outside world into the home and into the classroom and making much more of what came under the global term 'culture' available to a vast number of people, instead of only to those who had the means of transport and the money to avail themselves of the educational and cultural facilities provided by most of our cities.

Record players, tape recorders, cameras for still or motion-picture photography, in black and white or colour, are an accepted part of life in many homes where a high percentage have radio or television, and the number of children with their own transistor radios is legion. It follows that young people are not only familiar with the machines required for modern means of communication, but are capable of making their own tapes and combining media such as tape and film (to give pictures, commentary and music) with almost incredible ability.

It would appear that by no means all schools are preparing their pupils for the kind of world into which they will go and within which they will expect and be expected to play their part. Thirty years ago it was presumed that the child would learn more in the classroom than elsewhere and the teacher was regarded as the person solely responsible for teaching him. With the advent of radio and television, in particular, and their provision in schools, the teacher is no longer in control, for example, of the subject content of the material.

More than ever, therefore, it has become necessary that the teacher should re-examine his role so that in this three-cornered situation involving himself, the pupil and the new media he will see his part, vastly different as it must be, yet no less important than it ever has been. Team teaching, co-operative teaching, the integrated day, block timetables – whatever the new methods may be called – it is obvious that the teacher–teaching situation has changed. Making use of the strengths of individual teachers for the benefit of more pupils can at the same time free pupils from teachers' weaknesses.

One cannot think of the act of bringing together several classes of children to see a film, or to hear a radio broadcast, without thinking of the situations it will create. If four classes are watching a film, what are the teachers doing – particularly if the showing of the film is an annual event? Are they giving help to other pupils elsewhere? Are they assessing work already produced by these pupils and planning, as a result, further assignments for them? Are they considering necessary and appropriate change because the medium as first exploited has been unsuccessful with a particular pupil? Has the pupil's interest taken an unexpected turn? Time for analysis of this kind has to be found for teachers involved in planning structured individualized learning using the media to their fullest.

Experiences and ideas must be shared among pupils and teachers. New methods and techniques are not only breaking down classroom walls, but at the same time they are demanding a greater degree of organization because of the inter-involvement of staff and pupils from several classes.

As essential as the sharing of experiences and ideas is the sharing of resources within the school. These have to be looked at and considered as material owned by the school, rather than belonging to a particular teacher who may have been the one to suggest that the school should buy it in the first place. If the best use is to be made of the money available, and unnecessary and wasteful spending of money avoided, there will have to be a sharing of the resources. They must be recorded and located in such a way that access is freely available and hoarding no longer possible. Like all freedoms, this must be everyone's freedom with the respect and limitation which sharing demands.

Our personal collections of books in the home live together in a particular way because we, personally, use them that way – in certain groups for specific purposes: a chapter in this one, a paragraph in that. They form an approach which needs to be meaningful only to oneself. But books in classrooms, because they are used by many more people, are difficult to find unless they are arranged in a way that all members of the class understand is for ease in finding. This is necessary partly because each one who uses a book may do so for entirely different purposes from the others. Once the school library is started the problem becomes even more acute. It is at this stage that it becomes obviously necessary to have one member of staff who will be responsible for the organization and administration of the library, even if for no other reason than to act as arbitrator; he must be the unbiased one, with no axe to grind other than trying to ensure that the library functions to help everyone.

From an early age in school all children should be given instruction in the use of books and of a library. There is now, more than ever before, a basic educational discipline here which too often fails to be so recognized. The school library and its use is a vital part of the evolution of education, yet it is too often looked upon as something quite apart from or additional to it. 'He gets an allowance for looking after the library, so let him get on with it.' Most school librarians have heard that said. But the use of the school library is every teacher's responsibility; it is a tool as indispensable for the teacher as for the pupil. And, after all, it has to be organized by someone.

Modern educational methods, laying emphasis on the individual learning situation, inevitably require means of communication to be as varied as the needs and limitations of the learners. Not for everyone, and not for every situation, is the book the answer. A description on the page of a textbook on the working of a four-stroke engine may be understood by some; a colour film with sound, a coloured chart, a filmloop or a filmstrip with a taped commentary will be much more effective for those less accustomed to mechanical matters, or for those with reading difficulties for whom it is just possible that some means of conveying information other than through the printed word will provide the spark to motivate an interest in learning to read. The recorded sound of an actor speaking Shakespeare might well do much more for a pupil's appreciation and understanding of a play than either his own reading or that of his teacher.

The cassette tape, simple for most people to load and use, can be employed, for example, as the medium for the teacher to describe a pupil's assignment. It has the advantage of being spoken in a voice which he recognizes and it can be stopped, restarted and replayed any number of times for clarification or revision; this saves the teacher's time and makes it very much easier for the pupil who finds something difficult to follow but is reluctant to risk the teacher's irritation at having to repeat over and over again.

A pupil in the infant school may want to hear a favourite story. If he is not a fluent reader, or if he cannot read, should he ask or expect the teacher to stop what she is doing in order to tell him the story? Some children's stories are already on tape; it might be an advantage if the voice were his teacher's voice telling the story in her own way.

With network educational broadcasts it often happens that programmes are transmitted at a time which is too inconvenient for other work to be stopped in order to watch or listen. It is easier in the first and middle schools to fit in these broadcasts, but as pupils' specialization in subjects in secondary schools must be timetabled it becomes increasingly difficult. A taped broadcast, however, may be used at any convenient time, and a central collection of these in the library is a section which is likely to grow beyond the first conception of its usefulness.

The presence of a tape is like the presence of a book on any library shelf, so often consulted not because the reader was previously aware of its existence, but because he happened to see it as he was browsing. Commercially produced filmstrips and slides as well as those made by staff and pupils in the course of their school work, or presented by parents, will all find a place.

There will be charts and cut-outs from old books and periodicals; there will be posters and illustrations available free or at a small charge from many sources; there will be postcards, models, games, mathematical material and artefacts and specimens of all kinds. Perhaps these various items had been kept in classrooms or in cupboards, or in teachers' desks; perhaps many of the items were in the stockroom; perhaps some had already found their way into the library. And the biggest 'perhaps' of all: perhaps only a few teachers knew of relatively few of the items. Almost certainly there is a great deal of 'unknown' material in every school, the neglect of which does not justify the money and effort spent on acquiring it.

It is difficult to understand why there is opposition to the central control of resources – although the same situation obtained when the centralizing of library books was first suggested in schools which were at that time without a school library. It is likely that the individual teacher will gain immeasurably from having access to much more material by this arrangement. After all, if you refuse to lend what you have, do you have the nerve to ask and risk refusal when you want to borrow?

New developments bring their own quota of teething troubles and mistakes, but from these come further developments to strengthen and confirm the progress already made. Changing the name on the door of the stockroom does not make it a resource centre; this is probably the most short-sighted and serious mistake currently perpetrated by those more interested in bandwagons than education. 'Resource centre' is not just a new name for something which has been going on for a long time. The hardware and software may have been in the building for a long time; what is new is the concept of its use and the manner of recording and collocating to make it effective in an endless variety of situations with which the curriculum and individual learning are concerned.

In a way, the organization required for books in the school library to raise its potential value applies similarly to other media, yet the problem is made more difficult because of the nature of the newer materials. By and large we are accustomed to the book, to handling it, to perusing it, to consulting the index and to doing all this as we stand beside the bookcase. Not only will different senses be called into use, but also essential machines for consulting certain media; initially we are far from skilful in these situations, less skilful than the pupils themselves.

The individual reference or several references can easily be followed through when we seek material in a book, because we ourselves have been developing this kind of skill over a period of many years. How is the user helped when the material he seeks is in a frame somewhere in a forty-frame filmstrip? Or when the material is a single paragraph 'about halfway through' a large reel of tape? How difficult will this be, and how long will it be before it will be simple? Visual material is difficult to describe or transcribe, and the number of ways in which a single slide can be used varies almost with the number of people who have access to it. So it would appear that the documentation of non-book material available in the library may need to be much more detailed than the amount of analytical cataloguing provided in most traditional libraries.

The 'library resource centre' takes its place in any educational establishment as a modern extension of the library. Perhaps later we shall look back to the time when the term 'resource centre' was used to draw attention to the necessity, in individual learning situations, of material additional to books – with which the traditional library and the traditional librarian have been concerned for centuries. The professional librarian, whose training and expertise have equipped him to give so much assistance in the past, is well equipped to bring all this material together again.

Opportunities are available, and encouragement and assistance should be given to teachers with library responsibilities to acquire the knowledge that will make their task easier. Even so they cannot do it all alone. Pupils and teachers, by sharing their experiences, will be able to achieve approaches which could easily have been untouched or unrecognized by one individual.

Just as, twenty years ago, it was easy for teachers to be mesmerized and frightened by professional librarianship when they discovered what it involved, so there is a danger now that articles in the educational press will discourage many teachers from attempting this extension of the work of the school library. People, particularly the uninformed, can appear sophisticated in their talking and in their thinking, yet not all of them are practical in their doing. It will be a long time before the majority of schools will be affected by sophisticated techniques. It is so easy to talk about computers in libraries, about automatic data processing, and so on. Every head teacher knows how far the capitation allowance goes, and every teacher-librarian knows how little money is available for library books; we should have learned our lesson. Instead of yearning for tomorrow, let us be concerned with the present. Involved as we are with helping children to help themselves, and aware that there may be a very long road to walk before reaching the computers which we are told are just round the corner, there is much which can and should be attempted now.

The amount of money available for a head teacher to run his school is determined by the number and the ages of the pupils it contains; from this he has to allocate money for many items of which the library is only one. Even this share could be comparatively more generous than the time he is able to allocate for the teacher-librarian to be relieved from 'teaching' duties in order to establish and maintain an effective library. It is important, therefore, that the time the librarian does have is used to the best advantage and that, as far as possible, he should not have to make the same mistakes as many have made before him; no doubt he will make his own contribution in this particular field, for error is inherent in all new projects.

Few books have been published in the United Kingdom about 'resource centres', although America has been experimenting and writing about them for some time. A professional librarian in a nearby educational establishment, such as a school or college of further or higher education, can be a useful and mutually beneficial contact. It is usually helpful to see how others tackle the same kind of work even when there is a difference in the educational ability of those for whom it is provided. Whether such an exchange draws attention to one's own lack of knowledge or substantiates one's own procedures, the outcome should be productive.

It is possible that for some this whole project will appear too formidable to contemplate. In that case it is as well to remember that where professional librarianship is in action it is at least one librarian's work for the whole of a working day. The teacher-librarian has to come to terms with what he has the time and the assistance to tackle and what just cannot be attempted; he must match the standard he leads his colleagues to expect, and he must guard against the possibility of overwhelming himself so that in the end he proves the opposite of what he set out to do.

The author is aware of the pressures on teachers who look after school libraries and of the time which they give; in the following chapters some guidelines are offered in an attempt to minimize the burden which the introduction of non-book materials will inevitably bring. There are descriptions of some methods which have worked in different situations, together with alternative suggestions. Success lies in ensuring that what we devise does work in our own particular set of circumstances, and in allowing time for the users to become accustomed to a new kind of library.

CHAPTER TWO

The School Library

The use of books, and, developing with it, the use of libraries, cannot be considered in isolation since it continues through each successive stage in education. Taken together, these have to be seen as part of a development which is related not necessarily to the chronological age of those within each group, but rather to the experiences to which the individual members have previously been subjected. Both school and home are contributory factors in the environment, experiences and encouragement they provide. To some extent the presence of books in the home will probably depend on the attitude of at least one parent, but, when the quality of both the contents and the production of these books is considered, account must be taken of external factors for which the home cannot be held responsible.

Every bookseller is aware of the financial commitment involved in stocking books of a quality which those within his 'catchment area' are unable to appreciate, or even pay for. The lower the expected average reading age in that area, the greater the probability that there will not be a good bookshop nearby. An interest in those books that the local newsagent might stock could, at least, help to develop a fluency in reading which in itself is essential.

There may be a branch of the local public library, or a mobile library van may visit at intervals, but both these need the kind of sympathy and motivation for their use which may not be under the control of the individual who wants access to books. Parental agreement may be required and this may not be forthcoming for a variety of reasons. In a busy environment the interested parent may be unwilling to subject his child to the risks of heavy traffic. Both parents may be at work all day and have no time, be too tired or, because of library opening hours, too late to take the child to the library in the evening and unwilling to do so on a Saturday. Even when the reasons are no more than excuses, the child and the teacher may have to accept them.

It can be affirmed that those who use public libraries do so by choice, however this may be interpreted; and this statement is made in the shadow of annual statistics which show that a decided minority of the British population are members of public libraries. How different is the situation in schools where, among the children, there is a wide range of ability and where teachers are concerned with the individual development of each child, whether he can read or not and whether he wants to learn or not. Each school is unique because of its individual pupils and the group they form; because of the individual teachers and the community which they create; because of the head teacher with his interpretation of the curriculum and his decisions on the allocation of the capitation allowance.

Understandably, ideas have changed over the years and the present status of the school library and the realization and recognition of the part it can play in both primary and secondary education owe much to two factors in the immediate post-war years:

(a) the evolutionary development of primary education following the passing of the Education Act of 1944;

(b) the striking improvement in the quality and quantity of children's books.

Looking back, it is difficult to decide which came first, and difficult to imagine the progress of the one without the other. Both played an exciting and vital part in the growth and development of libraries in primary schools at a time when the Ministry of Education's Building Bulletins – No. 1 in 1945 and No. 2 in 1950 – were suggesting, for secondary schools, library standards given in area and number of rooms related to form entry, type of secondary education and sex of pupils, while no similar recognition appeared to be forthcoming for the needs of primary schools.

During this period, teaching methods in primary and secondary schools were so different as to draw attention to the need for an evaluation of the purpose and use of books in both sectors, to try to find a relationship between the two. Such a relationship did exist, but it had to be understood and both sectors had to be aware of it, for there was much confusion, as well as a considerable lack of imagination, surrounding the school library at each level. As it has turned out, it was the use made of the primary school library which pointed a way for the reappraisal of the philosophy of library provision in secondary education.

For long the grammar schools had seemed wedded to the idea of a library for the Vth and VIth forms in a room which often had to be used as a classroom, or else was a sanctum sanctorum with a bookstock geared to the examinations taken by those pupils. To refer to them as school libraries, as if they could rightly be assumed to be for the use of the whole school, was not, in fact, correct; yet the term was commonly used. It was encouraging when pupils newly transferred from primary schools with an active library sought permission to be allowed to continue using the primary school library. This signalled change.

Since secondary schools began to appoint professional librarians almost twenty years ago the provision has very gradually improved. Many librarians have come to this kind of librarianship through their interest in children's books and bring to these schools a refreshing insight and an appreciation of modern children's literature. They bring with them also their professional expertise to give a constant service to staff and pupils throughout each day.

However, not all secondary schools are large and not all the large ones have professional librarians on the staff full-time, even when a library room or a library suite has been provided in accordance with the regulations laid down by the Department of Education and Science. But still, it seems an odd situation that the provision of a science laboratory assumes the appointment of someone with science qualifications, the provision of a language laboratory assumes the appointment of someone with language qualifications, yet the provision of a library with valuable stock and a great need for professional expertise still appears to entail no similar assumption. And it is likely to be many years before comparable library provision will be made for British primary and middle schools.

Instead, the librarian is a teacher who may or may not have attended a course for teacher-librarians, but who will find sooner or later that the library will claim many more hours of his time than he can be allowed during the school day. No library functions efficiently of its own accord; where this impression is given it is certain that a great deal of work has gone into the planning of its organization and administration, that the necessary arrangements have been communicated to those who use it and that they, in their turn, are giving their support no matter how individualistic they would like to be.

Why have a library?

The question must be asked by primary and middle schools. Before routine procedures can be started there are initial important decisions to be made regarding its purpose.

'The scope of knowledge has become too vast to be covered extensively within the boundaries of classroom instruction, superior though that instruction may be. Through the school library these boundaries can be extended immeasurably in all areas of knowledge and in all forms of creative expression and the means provided to meet and to stimulate the many interests, appreciations and curiosities of youth.'[1]

[1] R. A. Davies, *The school library: a force for education excellence.*

In order to answer the basic question the following points seem to be the most important:

Is the library wanted to meet the needs of those pupils who do not have access to the public library?

Is the library to be used solely for reference in order to avoid the situation where the book that was borrowed yesterday is the book wanted, but not available, today?

Is the library going to lend fiction but not information books, and is this fair to those who are less interested in imaginative literature than in the world around them?

Problems like these must be faced and a great deal of help may be forthcoming from the children's and school library service of the local public library.

Where will the school library be located?

There seems to be no doubt nowadays that a central collection of books is essential and that there must be access to it throughout the school day. This collection should not, for example, be kept in the top classroom on the doubtful pretext that it will be used more there. The school hall, or some other area allowing freedom of access, would be better.

Some have experimented with books along corridors: this certainly expresses the belief that children should meet books wherever they go. It is a little difficult, however, to link this with the idea of a library as a working tool. Where a corridor arrangement was seen in a large new primary school it was obviously frustrating for many pupils who rushed or walked forlornly along corridors, upstairs and down, trying to find what they were looking for. Too much was being asked of too many children who were not on sufficiently familiar terms with books. Even so, it is possible for fiction books to be dealt with successfully using a corridor, so long as they are arranged in alphabetical order of authors.

However, with the growing change of attitude, from regarding the classroom as a box inhabited by a certain group for a term towards its being a room where a teacher operates with a specialization within a group-teaching framework, a room for the school library begins to have possibilities and to make sense. Here, perhaps, the teacher-librarian, undoubtedly with other responsibilities, can be more easily available in a fluid situation. This has been done with considerable imagination and flexibility and been successful.

Storage of books

Shelving provided against the walls of a room allows circulation space in the centre and gives the opportunity to use tables and chairs. This has not always been easy in the past because of radiators and windows, and sometimes it has been difficult to find wallspace to take the standard 3 ft (914 mm) wide bookcase. Now, with the contents of the library including materials which require access to a power point for the machine needed to listen to or view them, this particular problem has shifted its position. As power points are likely to be provided in existing schools around the walls, bookcases may have to project from the walls or else be set in the centre of the room in such a way that the sequence of the classification is not impeded (but see p. 47).

The generally accepted width of a library shelf is 3 ft (914 mm). Information books for children tend to be thinner than fiction books and thinner than books for adults. Placed normally on the shelf, thin books are inclined to slip easily with the resultant possibility of their building up vertically on top of one another and making it more difficult to find particular books as they are required; books lying on their sides are liable to have their spines damaged more easily because of the way they are retrieved.

A shelf 30 in (762 mm) wide is recommended, and for books not more than 10 in (254 mm) high the shelf should be 7–8 in (177–203 mm) from back to front. There are bound to be books over 10 in high; these are best shelved separately in a parallel arrangement allowing 14 in (356 mm) in height between one shelf and the next and with a depth of 10 in (254 mm).[1]

[1] The narrower shelves recommended are available from Terrapin Reska.

If it is proposed to use a spur type of shelving the temptation to use a long shelf should be avoided unless it has an upright at each end and enough supports to give a section not more than 30 in (762 mm) wide.

Some suppliers of library furniture stock wall shelving and free-standing runs of double-sided bookcases in a variety of heights, finishes and colours. Catalogues are usually available. Tables, chairs and carrels are also available from suppliers, although the local education authority may make its own provision.

CHAPTER THREE

Adding a Book

In broad outline, a book is selected, ordered, received, accessioned, classified, catalogued, processed, issued for loan, returned and eventually withdrawn from stock. Listed like this it all seems remarkably simple and perhaps a little dull. It is proposed to look in more detail at these stages, because a pattern of procedures should help the librarian to be methodical in a situation where the time at his disposal is seldom enough for the possibilities which a well organized school library can offer.

Book selection

It is not uncommon to find in the review of a book that it is considered suitable for, say, a boy 8–9 years old. Which boy of this age? Chronological age cannot be a yardstick since there is a complete range of ability within it, including those who cannot read.

It has been said that the school library should have only the best books on any subject. To ask what is meant by the best book, and for whom is it the best book, does not preclude consideration of standards in writing and production, or reliability of subject content, but it does imply that if we are to encourage the use of the library there has to be an initial point of contact which will motivate the potential user to come to the library. In considering these problems, the philosophy of R. A. Davies, expressed in the work already cited (p. 13), seems appropriate:

'The great advantage of the conception of equality of opportunity is that it candidly recognizes differences in endowment and motivation and accepts the certainty of differences of achievement. By allowing free play to these differences it preserves the freedom to excel which counts for so much in terms of individual aspirations and has produced so much of man's greatness . . . Having committed ourselves to equality of opportunity we must strive incessantly to make it a reality in our own society . . . If we are really serious about equality of opportunity we shall be serious about individual differences, because what constitutes opportunity for one man is a stone wall for the next. If we are to do justice to the individual we must seek for him the level and kind of education which will open *his* eyes, stimulate *his* mind and unlock *his* potentialities . . . But though the educational pattern may differ the goals remain the same for all, enabling each young person to go as far as his aptitudes will permit in fundamental knowledge and skills and motivating him to continue his own self-development to the full along similar lines.'

Bearing this in mind, the librarian's task is to sift through and interpret information about new books. Of course, book reviews are a useful source, but it may take the librarian a little time to learn the value of individual contributors in this field. Two reviewers may give opposing evaluations and in time the librarian will develop a sensitivity to the reliability of reviewers. At the same time, he will relate information received in this way to the range of abilities among the pupils of the school.

Apart from those which cater for subject specializations, four periodicals are worth the librarian's attention:

Children's Book Review
Children's Books Supplement of the *Times Literary Supplement*
Growing Point
The School Librarian

Membership of the School Library Association should be considered by every school; it has many branches throughout the country. The annual subscription covers the cost of *The School Librarian* periodical as well as allowing reduced rates for any of its other publications.

The school librarian should contact the local librarian in charge of the schools library service; this may reveal the existence of a permanent updated display of recent additions of books.

Ordering a book

The arrangements for ordering books vary from one local education authority to another and in some cases the books are processed before sending them to the schools. At this stage, however, the librarian should be beginning to develop some method of making one record of a book serve several purposes.

A printed, punched card,[1] 5 × 3 in (127 × 76 mm), as shown in Fig. 1, can start as a record of a book order, be added to through different processing stages and finish as a shelf list card. The accumulation of shelf list cards for all media arranged in classified order can take the place of the classified catalogue. If, at any time, the librarian is required to show an accessions register these cards can be re-arranged in accession order.

Of the items listed, the author's name, title, edition, year of publication, publisher and the standard book number, all are to be found on the front or reverse of the title-page of a book; these are the details which distinguish one title from another.

It is almost inevitable that in any printed card or pro-forma designed for a particular use there will be sections which are un-

[1] Available from Don Gresswell Ltd.

necessary when the card is used for a different purpose; in this case the sections 'Requested by' and 'Source' can be put to other uses when the card is used as a guide for voluntary typists preparing catalogue cards. (Figure 8, p. 81, shows a suggested pro-forma for non-book materials.) For reasons which are explained later, it would be an advantage to have the accession number under the classification number, and as 'No. of copies' is not applicable this may be ruled through.

Class number	Author (surname first)			
No. of copies	Title			
Date ordered				Volumes
Of	Edition	Year	Publisher	Price
Order number	Requested by			
	Source			
		S.B.N.		
				D.G.Ltd. N.21. Cat. No. 2801.

Fig. 1

The bibliographic details are now inserted into the spaces on the card and an order is despatched according to the authority's arrangements.

Of course, books are not always wanted because they have just been published, but bibliographic details will still have to be found. These can be checked in the local public library, if the branch is not too small. Two reference books are useful in this respect:

Whitaker's *British books in print*. This is now published

annually in two volumes in alphabetical order of authors, titles and subjects.

The British National Bibliography. A weekly periodical, this was started in 1950 and lists, in Dewey Decimal Classification order, new books and new editions as they are published. Later they are issued in this order in accumulated forms and also in alphabetical order of authors, titles, subjects, series, etc. The BNB number appears as part of the entry in the latter arrangement. The classification number is also given, so the full entry can be traced, but it is important that the librarian should remember that this number should be no more than a starting point in his consideration of the placing of the book; otherwise he may find himself with some strange placings. The BNB only classifies books as separate units; there is no attempt to link books so that they form a library.

Books on order

The cards for all books on order are retained by the librarian. They can be kept in alphabetical order of authors or titles or else in date sequence so that, in time, the outstanding orders will come to the front. If a publisher cannot immediately meet an order he will send his reason to the supplier who should notify the school; this reason should be noted in pencil on a convenient part of the form, so that the librarian is aware of the state of the order. A month is long enough to wait before chasing the supplier. It is likely that books ordered in one financial year, if undelivered in that year, will be charged against the allowance for the year in which they are delivered.

Receiving into stock

Using a date stamp, neatly date the card with the date of receipt of the book, and date the order book entry at the same time.

Have a rubber stamp made showing the name of the school.

Three rows of lettering can be fitted into a stamp half an inch (13 mm) deep. There is no need to have obtrusive notices on books so long as they are clear; the same stamp may be used to identify a slide, or for a self-adhesive label to fix on the outside of a filmstrip container. Stamp the lower part of the title-page.

If the stamp does not have a knob to indicate the way to hold it to make an impression the right way up, then, with a penknife, remove a small slice of wood from the handle so that when the index finger touches the flat part of the wood it means that the stamp is the right way up.

Accessioning

The accession number is the one piece of information about a book which distinguishes it from every other book in the library, including another copy of the same title (which will have an accession number of its own). It used to be customary, and in many authorities mandatory, to keep an accessions register which was a record of all books as they were received, in chronological order. This was of no real use and, as far as the librarian was concerned, was an unnecessary duplication of another record which had to be made in the catalogue. Some used the accessions register for checking stock, but that must have been the most cumbersome and time-consuming exercise ever invented. However, although methods have changed, accessioning still has to be done, and done with care, for mistakes are easily made.

If, as seems natural, one starts with the figure 1, as the stock increases the number will grow from one to two, three and probably four digits. But by starting at 1001 one keeps a constant four-figure number, allowing a great deal of numerical space before having to be concerned about five figures.

Keep an exercise book to record each accession number as it is used; it acts as a check book to ensure that each item about to be numbered takes its sequential place in the addition of stock, and it is the simplest way for the librarian to remind himself of the last number used. In a book this number is put on the reverse of the title-page, as near the centre of it as space allows and with enough space below it for the classification number to be inserted later. The title-page is less likely to disappear than any other and is not removed when the book is sent for rebinding.

Classification and cataloguing

These processes, normally carried out at this stage, are discussed in Chapters 6 and 7. When they have been done there will be, in addition to the shelf list card, either catalogue cards, catalogue strips, or both, accompanying the book for the remaining procedures.

Issue system

It may be decided that books must not leave the library, although this is not likely if fiction books are kept in the library. For one reason or another books are likely to be borrowed sometime and for every book borrowed from the library a record must be left in the library. For the librarian's peace of mind this golden rule has to be established. The easier the librarian makes it the more likelihood there will be of its being regarded: there is no point in being idealistic about this.

The librarian will be aware of at least one issue system but it may not be the most convenient for his library.

1. *Photo-charging* is not likely to be possible on financial grounds; if it were it is more than likely that the librarian would use such finance to buy other materials for the library.

2. The *Browne charging system* is still widely used. A card showing the author's name, the title of the book, its accession number and classification number is made out for each book. The card with these details is inserted into a pocket pasted into the book. When the book is borrowed the card is transferred into one of a number of pocket-like tickets given to each borrower;

this record is held by the library as long as the book is on loan. When the book is returned the card is put back into the book and the reader is given his ticket.

If this system is used, the librarian must make sure that each pupil has a realistic number of tickets. The decision also has to be made whether the borrower keeps his own unused tickets, with the risk that he loses them, or whether unused tickets are kept by the librarian, with the disadvantage that they are not easily available to the borrower.

3. There is a third method gaining favour which avoids the use of tickets as described. There are two variations of this method, both making use of a card 5 × 3 in (127 × 76 mm), the same size as the standard catalogue card. One system uses a card *for each book,* which the borrower signs when he borrows the book; the other uses a card *for each borrower,* in which he enters the titles of borrowed books.

An issue card for each book

A pocket $3\frac{1}{4}$ × $2\frac{3}{4}$ in (82 × 70 mm) is pasted into the inside front cover of each book. The card bears the author's name and the title and accession number of the book in either of the forms shown in Figs 2 and 3. The two top pieces of information should also appear on the pocket for simplification in discharging the issue.

With the author's name at the top and the arrangement of the issue alphabetically by author (either straight through or behind a date) it is a simple matter to trace a book which may be wanted. If the accession number is at the top then, when a book has to be traced in the issue, the accession number has first to be found; this could involve consulting the name catalogue for the classification number and then the shelf list card for the accession number.

Using the card in this way, the reader need add in writing only his name and probably his class. The author has experience of this system over a period of nine years and it proved simple and effective.

A card for each borrower

Although this method is simple to set up, as cards only have to be typed for each pupil (Fig. 4), or handwritten by the pupil himself or the teacher, it does later lead to problems. The librarian must satisfy himself that he has answers to the following questions:

AUTHOR	SERRAILLIER
TITLE	1234 The Trojan horse

Date	Name

DG 1301

Fig. 2

Will pupils be limited to one piece of material on loan?

Will pupils be limited to borrowing only books?

Will all pupils have the same number of cards? If not, who will decide the quantity for each?

Who will keep the cards? If it is not the librarian then he may well have a few queries to deal with during the course of a year.

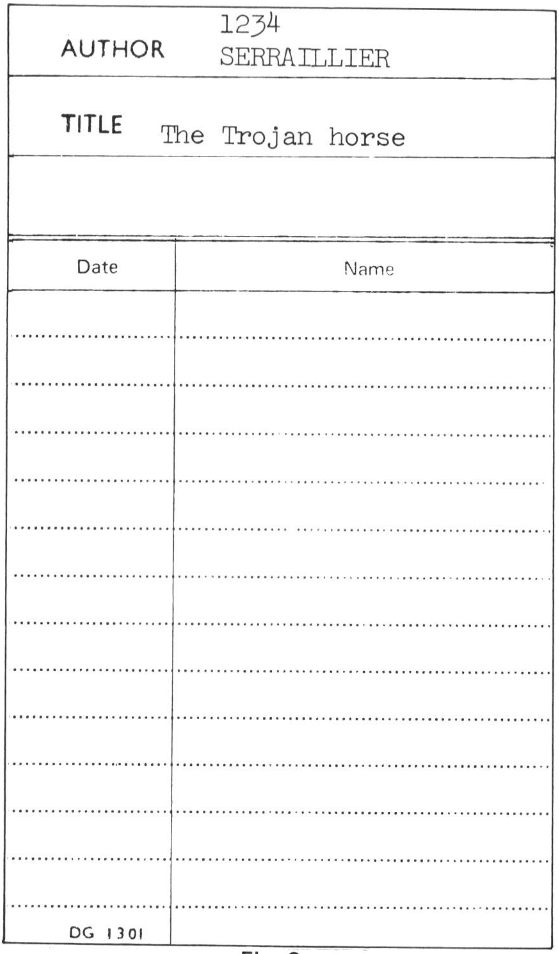

AUTHOR	1234 SERRAILLIER
TITLE	The Trojan horse

Date	Name
DG 1301	

Fig. 3

Will all pupils be competent to enter on the card the title of the books that they are borrowing? If they are not, is it in fact good practice that it should be done by them?

The answers to these questions will, of course, depend on the context in which they are asked. They have been set out like this to ensure that the librarian appreciates the need for basic decisions to be made before various systems are introduced.

NAME	Peter Robinson
FORM	2 a

Date	Title
....	....
....	....
....	....
....	....
....	....
....	....
....	....
....	....
....	....
....	....
....	....
....	....
DG 1302	

Fig. 4

As far as the teacher is concerned, it is important to remember that no card system can act as a faithful guide to what a pupil reads. In the author's experience, the only way to find out what a pupil has read is to ask him. This is an important way for both teacher and librarian to find out why some books fail to keep the attention of the pupil. The information gathered will help book selection in the future. It is salutary to remember one's own reactions both as a child and as an adult. The path of English literature is strewn with horses led to water ...

The size of tray required for this size of issue card is illustrated in Plate 1, which shows an open tray with alphabetical guide cards and a cabinet which can close to exclude dust.

Date labels

There is no pressing need to use date labels, especially in the close relationship which exists between pupils and teachers in the primary school. If they are felt to be necessary they should be pasted into the front of the book (to face the pocket which is on the inside of the front cover). In this position the thickness of the pages of text underneath takes the pressure used in date-stamping. Because of the risk of damage to the spine, the label should not be attached to the outside cover of the book.

An up-to-date bookstock

At best it is unimaginative to believe that once a book is added to stock it must always remain; this is the kind of attitude which might well sign the library's death warrant. No library can be judged solely on the number of books it possesses, but it can be judged by the suitability and condition of its stock for the educational purposes it is intended to fulfil.

It must be accepted that in a well-used primary or middle school library there will be a turnover of 15–20 per cent of stock every year. In other words, for every £100 allocated for books for the library £15–20 will be required for replacements. The

Plate 1   (a) Issue box (b) Issue tray (c) School name embossing stamp

librarian should not keep on his shelves out-of-date books or books which he finds distasteful to handle; if the book is too dirty for him, it is too dirty for the pupils. They, in turn, should be trained to report damage so that books are not returned to the shelves with loose pages or with damage to the binding, either of which can easily be repaired.

Safeguarding the appearance of the bookstock

Publishing houses pay a great deal of attention to the design of bookjackets which, outwardly, make an individual item out of each title. With their colourful appearance they have given libraries an appeal they lacked for too long. Unless steps are taken to preserve them, however, they can be the first outward signs of a neglectful librarian. There is no reason why librarians should retain bookjackets which are dirty and torn. One thing that the teacher and the librarian have in common is the fact that much that they do is there for all to see. Whatever standard each may profess to have, the real standard is always on display.

Transparent plastic covering for bookjackets

Small quantities of transparent adhesive covering, protected with a paper backing until ready to be used, can be bought from the better stationers.

In rolls of 27 yards (25 m) and in varying widths from $9\frac{1}{2}$–$19\frac{1}{2}$ in (241–495 mm), this material is available under the trade names 'Vistafoil GB' and 'Takibak'.[1]

Strengthened bindings

Many books for children are available from certain suppliers in strengthened bindings which give longer wear than the same books coming from the publisher direct.[2] After having been

[1] Available from Don Gresswell Ltd and G. Blunt and Sons, respectively.
[2] Catalogues of fiction and information books of this type are issued by one such company, Junior Books.

given a strengthened binding the books have the bookjackets heat-sealed with a transparent covering and attached to the books. Not only is the life of the book lengthened but its appearance remains bright and attractive for a long time, and all at little more than the original cost of the book.

CHAPTER FOUR

The Librarian and His Helpers

The librarian

Books may have come to be part of the library stock for a variety of reasons, not all of which were necessarily connected with curricular activities, in the classroom sense of the word; but the reason for the presence of slides, filmstrips, models, pictures, etc., in the school is almost certain to indicate that they were bought as a teaching aid for a particular piece of work. So as the library stretches forward to extend its functions to include a variety of media it does so to a good start for it is already essentially curriculum-based.

This extension of the library's function brings together teaching/learning aids to make the library the information centre for the school: collecting information and arranging it so that it can be easily and quickly retrieved is what the multi-media resource centre is about. The librarian's job is to examine the media received, looking for relationships between one part and another; when these are found he makes them known through the subject groupings of the materials themselves and through the records he puts into the catalogue. The service he gives is for the school as a whole, as is the contribution of individual teachers.

Librarianship is not, and has never pretended to be, about the making of audio-visual aids, so it cannot be about the making of films, filmstrips, slides, tapes or any combination of these or any other media.

Librarianship is not, and has never pretended to be, about the maintenance and repair of the machines required for viewing or listening to a variety of media; about running off fifty copies of a poem or anything else that the teacher who wants it is just as able to do for himself; about teaching or learning techniques.

It would have been salutary if there had been less haste in certain quarters of education, not least among teachers in charge of audio-visual aids, to make erroneous or meaningless statements about librarianship. Education has provided at least its quota of howlers. The introduction of professional librarianship into educational establishments provided an early 'I catalogue my library by a modified Dewey' which was thought to be unsurpassable. Yet in 1971 there appeared in print: 'A weakness of a system such as the Dewey indexing system is that it gives the title of a book or article without providing any information about its contents'. That was a turn-up for the books if ever there was one. A previous indiscretion from the same source was concerned about the librarian having enough to do to 'log and issue books, etc.'.

This seems unfortunate, because those interested in the production and use of audio-visual aids have such a valuable contribution to make towards the success of the modern library; it is unfortunate, too, that often those who hear such statements believe them. When administrative decisions are based on such crude statements as these and when there has been no check with the profession concerned it is little wonder that librarians continue to have to spend too much valuable time on mopping-up operations.

It may be that the librarian is a creative artist in some of the media mentioned and that he has educational qualifications and experience similar to those of his teaching colleagues. But two facts must be borne in mind:

1. If he is appointed as a librarian, his responsibility and his authority rest in librarianship.
2. If he is really doing the job as it should be done it is extremely unlikely that he will have time, or even the inclination, to be involved other than through librarianship.

The librarian has a special contribution to make to the life and work of the school. In a large secondary school there may be a professional librarian on the staff; his responsibility will be solely in connection with the library. Any teaching he does will be in explaining the use of the library and of books and most of this will probably be with individual users as they seek or are given help.

Other secondary schools and middle and primary schools will be without professional expertise of this kind. In these instances a teacher is asked or may offer to look after the library. If it is at all possible the teacher should be encouraged to attend library classes or, at the very least, to attend meetings of the nearest branch of the School Library Association.

A teacher with three years' teaching experience can study for the teacher-librarian certificate; an enquiry to the School Library Association will tell him where a course is being run. Not only does such a course give the teacher-librarian information about, and practical experience in, some of the work, but it gives him a contact with other teachers who may be experiencing the same difficulties as himself. It is so easy for a teacher doing this work to imagine that he is the only one with difficulties and problems.

Teacher-librarian or librarian – the term does not matter. Professional librarian or not, the person in charge of the library is still the librarian. If he is not a professional librarian then the library is probably only part of his daily responsibilities and he is the one this book is trying to help; as far as possible he should be helped to avoid falling into the traps prepared for the unsuspecting by the uninformed by means of the educational press. Where the library has a good foundation he should not find it difficult to make the new step towards expansion, but where this is lacking he will be wise to re-organize the books side before accepting new material.

In this new situation in which he finds himself the librarian will need to use his imagination; if he is able to visualize the kinds of opportunity which the modern school library should offer he will know that he needs all sorts of help to make it work effectively. In his enthusiasm he should guard against leading those who will use the library to expect it to do more than he can quickly provide; in selling the idea he must be careful not to oversell. It is better to be in a position where he can continue to improve the service he gives than to start with impressive promises only to find that time is against him and he has to withdraw from the ground he had gained.

Centralization

While acknowledging the unwillingness to hand over equipment acquired over the years, there can be few teachers who would not admit the advantage of having access to more teaching/ learning aids. There is never likely to be enough money to give every teacher all that he would like to have, particularly since, in each classroom, equipment which would almost certainly be wanted by colleagues would be lying unused for at least part of each term.

Centralizing materials gives an opportunity to buy in a way that allows greater variety for the money available and that avoids unnecessary duplication. With luck the public library may have a display of useful materials. Plate 2 shows some of the items on display in the School Library Service of Wiltshire County Library. In addition to the books, slides, filmstrips, pictures, records and models seen here, there are films, charts, posters, postcards, aerial photographs and archives. Other services and advice are available to teachers for the asking. This is the kind of help which is sometimes available and it is up to the librarian to enquire about local facilities; when he knows what is available he can inform his colleagues and put a card in the catalogue drawer.

Plate 2   Multi-media display. School Library Service, Wiltshire County Library

Accessibility

To decide on access to materials in the modern library is not easy but the decision has to be made at the outset because a number of other factors will rest on it. It is difficult basically because we are new to the media, and their place in education, in the general learning situation, is less obvious than that of the book. The decision is not made any easier for the teacher who knows that some local education authorities will not allow teachers to handle audio-visual equipment until they have attended a course and have a signed certificate stating that they are proficient, yet, at the same time, children in some infant schools make considerable use of tape recorders, and slide and filmstrip projectors.

There has to be access in individualized learning situations. There may have to be precautions and there will have to be training, but we have to be realistic about the pupils involved; their experience may well differ from that of their teachers. Access to slides, filmstrips and the machines necessary for their use may be new as far as the school experience of the pupil is concerned, but may be part of his normal home environment. He may have his own record player and his own precious records so what he is doing in school may not be anything new – more than one nine-year-old has threaded an 8 mm film into a projector when the teacher was making no headway.

Since the retrieval of information will be possible through more than one medium, the necessary machines for viewing all the media must be available in the library, in addition to any machines made available for use in classrooms. To make this work, decisions will have to be made about access to material. This may involve the reference use only of material held in the library but there should be no serious problem if actual, rather than hypothetical, situations are faced. A filmloop projector placed in the library is freed as soon as the user finishes projecting and someone else can follow on with his filmloop immediately. In an active library it is inconvenient when a filmloop projector is removed for several hours at a time and used for six minutes of that period; neither colleagues nor pupils should have to go searching for equipment.

It is a poor library which does not arouse enthusiasm, provoke excitement or produce industrious activity. The investigations involved in working through an assignment, and the satisfaction when it has been completed; the excitement of discovering a piece of information which is of personal interest or which can be shared with another member of the group who will use it to fulfil his share of the assignment; the satisfaction of finding a reproduction of a painting which appeals, of listening to a recording of poetry, of listening to a favourite story well told, of enjoying congenial music: all these will be there, together with the liveliness of discussion around individual contributions to a piece of group work, and the warmth of shared experiences.

It is rather like using a bank account in that, unless the material goods are there, there will be nothing to withdraw. But although the total amount of available material may not in the first instance be great, this is not necessarily a drawback and can even be an advantage for the less able pupil. The unaccustomed success of the hitherto slow learner gives him a new role. Because the use of a new medium has shed some light and he is no longer dependent on the printed word, he is no longer laughed at or ignored. New attitudes to learning will be born and the librarian will be in the centre of the change so he will need the co-operation of his colleagues to ensure that everyone will have the same opportunities to benefit.

Reference use

When classes met behind closed doors it was usual for books to be borrowed in bulk from the central collection for use in classrooms for project work; this produced a certain amount of inaccessibility when they were retained long after they were needed. Now that classroom doors have metaphorically been removed it has become more usual for those pupils who require access to resources, whether these be materials or teachers, to go to the place where they are to be found. With team or co-operative teaching in progress the teacher in charge of the library would perhaps occupy the library to provide a presence and, by implication, supervision. This might be the answer for many schools using modern approaches and trying to centralize materials, for, with a little imagination, the library could provide considerable motivation for active participation by all with access to it.

Help for the librarian

Help from pupils

There are two principal ways in which this is given. The pupil will be asked for help by the librarian, who has noticed his interest in the library; this request may come via his teacher, at the instigation of the librarian. Alternatively, the pupil himself will offer the kind of help he thinks he can give.

When the librarian asks for help in pasting pockets inside books, for example, he has to set his standards and see that they are kept. (This may, in fact, be a service which the local education authority already gives.) The librarian might ask that two pupils from each class be made responsible for keeping a particular bookcase tidy, or the filmstrips, or cassette tapes. Responsibility for tidiness usually results in a wary eye being kept on defaulters. Basically this is not a bad thing, but the librarian should try to stress that the helper's pride in the ability of others to find material within the area for which he is responsible is more important than the role of sergeant-major in which the pupil could so easily see himself.

This kind of contribution is extremely valuable. It involves the ability of the pupil to recognize by means of the classification notation each item's correct place in the scheme and so detect the items which wander. Pupils with this kind of ability will be spotted down the school so that, with training by the librarian, there will be a constant supply. Let them be known as library helpers, assistant librarians, library assistants or any other title which will denote their connection with the librarian. Too much enthusiasm can be a nuisance if material is forever being put in its correct place, but the librarian will be able to judge how often this need be done and which time of day is best.

There are pupils who are aware that some duties are beyond them, yet they want to help. Others make an offer and, when they find it accepted, almost long for the work to be endless. They offer, perhaps, to arrange the issue for fiction books on loan or to remind those who have forgotten to return material. They can be made responsible for collecting from staff old papers to be used as a base for pasting illustrations on mounts. There may be offers to tidy and dust. Many pupils derive much satisfaction from their ability to give the kind of help which has received no recognition in the classroom. Whatever method they adopt to express their pride, it should either be accepted as offered or a way found to channel it into a more appropriate form.

Help from colleagues

Colleagues can give a special kind of help in that they can suggest suitable additions to stock, although these may have to be considered *in toto* so that estimates are not exceeded. They can view new material when it arrives to suggest possible uses, and in this way can help the librarian to make adequate catalogue entries by informing him of the whereabouts of useful related information or material, e.g. a poem or selection of poems illustrating a particular theme, or a particular illustration in a book in the library. This kind of recording was not normally done in the traditional school library.

The greatest assistance which colleagues can give is practical support for the arrangements which the librarian makes to try to ensure that the new enterprise runs smoothly. At any time the librarian's task is difficult but it is eased if every teacher offers generous support.

Help from parents

On the whole, British schools are not quick to enlist the help of parents who could give considerable assistance to the librarian desperately in need of it. Somewhere among the parents there may be a typist who could copy-type relevant details from the pro-forma which the librarian completes when he classifies and catalogues additions to stock (see Fig. 8, p. 81). It may be possible to allow access to a school typewriter at certain times, or the work could be taken home.

There may be an amateur photographer who would copy slides – so long as copyright is not broken – or photograph charts (see p. 118), or who would talk to pupils about the use of cameras. There may be helpers willing to cut out and mount pictures. There may be a keen woodworker who could make or help to make equipment too costly to purchase when the initial need is for materials (see plans for carrel (fig. 5)). And think of all the parents longing to be asked to assemble plastic model kits!

Some parents may work in offices where envelopes with interesting foreign stamps are normally consigned to the wastepaper-basket; here is another source of help. It is not difficult to find, as can be seen in the two British stamps shown in Colour Plate 1, statements of fact which are not only visually and historically interesting but also call for comparison and investigation beyond and apart from the fact that they happen to appear on postage stamps.

Parental interest in industrial archaeology could produce an item such as the London and South Western Railway signal finial shown in Colour Plate 4; a father might find unexpected interest in seeing the pictures and the historical and creative writing likely to result from its appearance in school. Grandparents, too, may be able to help by giving up hoarded items of local material like the bottles shown in Colour Plate 4; compared with the ten thousand different types found in one year, this is a minute collection. Depending on the nature of local industry, different areas will provide different objects of interest, and pupils may have the opportunity to record on tape and film the history of their use as recalled by older members and friends of the family circle.

There is so much help waiting to be found. Much has been suggested which could release the librarian to do the work or provide the kind of help which only he is in a position to do. It is important that the librarian should not be so immersed in the kind of involvement shown above that his real function is lost. The librarian is in a unique position since he is the only one who handles all material for classification and cataloguing, and this gives him the opportunity to be aware of inter-media relationships beyond those that appear in the catalogue.

CHAPTER FIVE

Preparations for Assembling Materials

Before seeking agreement to have teaching/learning aids centralized the librarian should try to decide which kinds he proposes to include, and which to omit. For example, it may be that overhead transparencies are personal to the work of a particular teacher who is unwilling to make his own work communal property. While this is perfectly understandable, it will not preclude their incorporation in principle and should not in any case apply to material purchased with school money.

The librarian should have planned how he proposes to receive the individual items which will make up this part of the library, how he will organize them when they have been received and, above all, how he is going to allow the freedom of access which each teacher already enjoys for the material at present in his classroom. The argument of commonsense economics about unused materials may not have much appeal until everything is in action and unexpected resources have started to appear. He will have to find out how much he can expect and then perhaps have to decide how much he can accept from what has been offered.

Both in the primary and the middle school the librarian is bound to have a rough idea of what is in the school, and he will certainly know that if there is not a Super 8 mm filmloop projector it is unlikely that there will be Super 8 mm filmloops. He should prepare a list to include films, filmstrips, filmloops, slides, reel-to-reel and cassette tapes, records, overhead transparencies, maps, globes, models, games and any other media which may be available. The list can be duplicated, with a space to the left of each medium for the individual teacher to insert the quantity that he holds, and a copy can then be given to each colleague and to the head teacher, who may have material in his room or who may be responsible for what is in the stock room, and one copy kept for a total.

Once the librarian is in a position to assess the extent of the participation there are three ways in which he can approach the task.

1. He can ask for all materials to be sent to him by a certain date. It is wise to assume that everyone will immediately co-operate, in which case probably more equipment will arrive than the librarian can deal with quickly, and it may lie around for quite a long time. This would be a dangerous start.

2. He can deal with one classroom at a time. One teacher at a time will hand over immediately all that he has offered. Using this method it will always be difficult for individual teachers to know where things are, apart from their own.

3. He can ask for one medium at a time from all teachers, e.g. call in all filmstrips and all filmstrip notes. If the latter are not available or are disintegrating, fresh copies can be ordered from the supplier. When these have been added to stock, i.e. are classified, catalogued, processed and on the shelves, it will be time to ask all teachers for the slides they hold and any notes which accompany them.

The third suggested method is the most satisfactory. Teachers will know that if their filmstrips have been handed over to the librarian then all filmstrips are to be found with him. The librarian will be able to work through one particular medium with its individual processing and begin to learn its potential within the concept of the modern library. He may also realize, of course, how little of that potential he can put into effect until he organizes help with other duties.

The librarian should ensure that he is in fact ready to work on a medium before he asks for it. Before he asks for illustrations he must have the card for those which need mounts; local purchase can probably produce the card speedily but more time will have to be allowed if it has to be ordered through the local education authority supplies department. That process can take a long time. He may need plastic containers[1] for tapes, or mounts[2] for filmstrips which have to be cut up.

From material in his own classroom the librarian should prepare samples of a mounted illustration, slide, filmstrip or any other medium to be processed, taking great care to produce attractive examples with catalogue and subject index entries. These can be shown to teachers so that they can see the kind of service to which they will be contributing.

Integration

Those who are suddenly attracted by unfamiliar concepts tend, in their enthusiasm, to be infected with the jargon of a long-established process without understanding the significance of the phrases they use. Every profession has its jargon and librarianship is no exception; however, librarianship is exceptional in that it is assumed to be understood by a great many people whose apparently authoritative pronouncements have a somewhat hollow ring.

In order to correlate information in the library, integration is essential. That is a simple statement as it stands. Unfortunately, misunderstandings arose when the integration of information became confused with the integration of materials. At this stage commonsense might have prevailed but when the urge to elucidate took over one began to hear pronouncements like 'Materials must be integrated on the shelves with the books', and 'Materials must be integrated on the shelves with the books so that there will be books, slides, filmstrips, pictures, all together'. It is difficult to believe that this view was advocated by

[1] Available from EMI and Philips.
[2] Available from Diana Wyllie Ltd.

Plate 3
Multi-media
subject
display

someone actively engaged in the processes of information retrieval. Try to imagine this kind of integration in an active library where material would be constantly consulted and therefore moving to and fro on the shelves. Imagine twenty books, four tapes (three small and one large), two filmstrips, a mounted illustration 15 × 18 in (381 × 457 mm) and, interspersed singly between them, six slides, three records and two rolled 30 in (762 mm) charts. It is not only impracticable, it would probably damage valuable material. Plate 3 shows a display consisting of roughly twelve books, three filmstrips, eleven slides, four records, a railway map, a large photograph, a model railway engine and tender on rails and a lamp. (The filmstrip and slide viewers had better be kept out of the problem at this stage.) This is a display; now try to put it on a shelf. Now imagine the materials listed above in a bookcase, then the sum total of the library arranged similarly.

Can you see a harassed teacher prodding between one item and another, coping with charts protruding from shelves like hurdles and murmuring 'The slide must be here somewhere because the catalogue says so'? If this is really what is meant by integration then one can understand the diffidence of school librarians. Such 'integration' would also be asking too much of those expected to use this material, so that there is a fair chance that they would prefer to store things in the backs of drawers in classrooms.

Difficulties do arise with tape–slide combinations, slide sets, filmstrip–cassette combinations, and so on. With the use of the types of box shown in Plate 4 such combinations can become free-standing units. The older and the more able the pupil the easier it may be for him to manage, but it still must be remembered that many primary and middle school pupils have reading difficulties and with this group non-book materials play an important role.

The slow and non-readers have to be catered for and their enthusiasm matched if attention is to be held. To keep each medium self-contained as far as possible may be the best way; it saves having to sift through unwanted material for what is wanted. For many it is simpler to have the media segregated and clearly labelled; the seeming inconvenience of so many parallel sequences is less confusing than the multiplicity of types of information carriers.

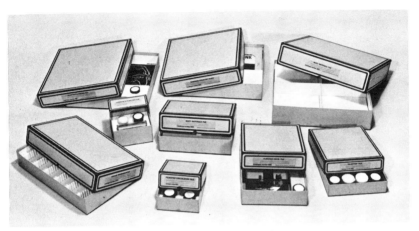

Plate 4   Containers for combinations of materials

Equipment for viewing and listening

In primary and middle schools it is likely that machines will be simple. It is not the purpose of this book to discuss the relative merits of individual items of equipment but rather to mention the kind of equipment most likely to be found in such schools. It is for each school to decide whether it is better for teachers and pupils to buy an expensive reel-to-reel tape recorder rather than a cassette tape recorder and two cassette playback-only machines; and whether the tape recorder will be battery or battery–mains. But places have to be found for what is acquired. If proximity to power points is essential then this may influence the siting of individual media.

Slide and filmstrip projectors need only be used for group viewing; if both are combined in the one machine perhaps only one such machine may be needed in the library, while any other similar projector could be movable within the school. The less the machines are moved about the better, so it would help if a screen were conveniently placed in relation to it; any kind of white surface will do – a large sheet of white card, or a white painted section of a wall. A small rear projection screen is also a possibility.

For individual viewing there are three useful possibilities:

1. *A lightbox with a magnifier*, such as the Kaiser shown in Plate 3 or a wooden box containing two small fluorescent tubes behind a translucent screen, is an effective way of looking at slides and also filmstrips. If a box is used there are many possibilities for different sizes and different methods of storage. For example, a long narrow box could be made which would stand in front of the slide-boxes and be able to take a wide row of single slides. On the other hand, a box about the same size as the slide-box could be used and stored with the slide-box, in which case it may be necessary to have more than one box.

2. *Battery powered viewers.* This is the only kind which is of any use in some circumstances, such as when there is no power point available nor access to sufficient daylight. These viewers suffer from the familiar disadvantage of unexpectedly exhausted batteries.

3. *Daylight viewers.* These handviewers vary in price from the Hanimex Hanorama three-dimensional viewer down to the simple ones at one-sixth of the price. Half-a-dozen of the cheaper ones means access to slides for six people rather than for only one.

In so far as finding space is concerned, the Super 8 mm filmloop projector is probably the least troublesome, partly because the inside of the lid can be used as a screen. Where space is at a premium it is possible to make a carrel using the top of an existing table or desk and without damaging it. Examples are shown in Fig. 5. If care is taken with the measurements it will slip over the sides of the desk or table and can be moved only up or down. The carrel excludes some of the light and serves as a fixed location for certain pieces of equipment. Again, this needs to be near a power point.

Central record of material

'Well, no. The library has a record of what I keep and anyone who wants it knows where to come.' There will be certain material that is required permanently in classrooms, but not as much as is claimed by some colleagues. Acquisitiveness is not always educationally sound.

There are two aspects of the usefulness or otherwise of keeping in the library a record of all material of information value in the school. In keeping a central record incorporated into the catalogue there is an underlying assumption that anyone who wants one of the items will know where to find it when the library is not the holding-point. That is the theory: in practice it does not work quite that way. Anyone who has worked in this situation knows that not only does such material tend to move around, but also that a record of its movements is seldom kept so that when it is wanted (because it is listed in the catalogue) it can be difficult to find someone who knows its whereabouts. The catalogue is provided to give positive statements concerning the stock and as the librarian has no control over this kind of material the validity of its inclusion in the catalogue is doubtful.

There is, however, a usefulness in keeping a central record, separate from the catalogue; this can be consulted by staff to reduce the risk of duplicate ordering of materials which relate to the function of the library. The librarian must be quite clear that it is no part of his function to be responsible for the supply of paper, pencils, chalk, brooms or any other type of equipment merely because of the use of the phrase 'central record'.

Accessioning

Book accessioning has been dealt with in Chapter 3, and although there is no reason to do other than incorporate the new media with the books it may be useful to look at the ways in which this can be done.

1. *Single sequence of numbers.* Irrespective of medium, items

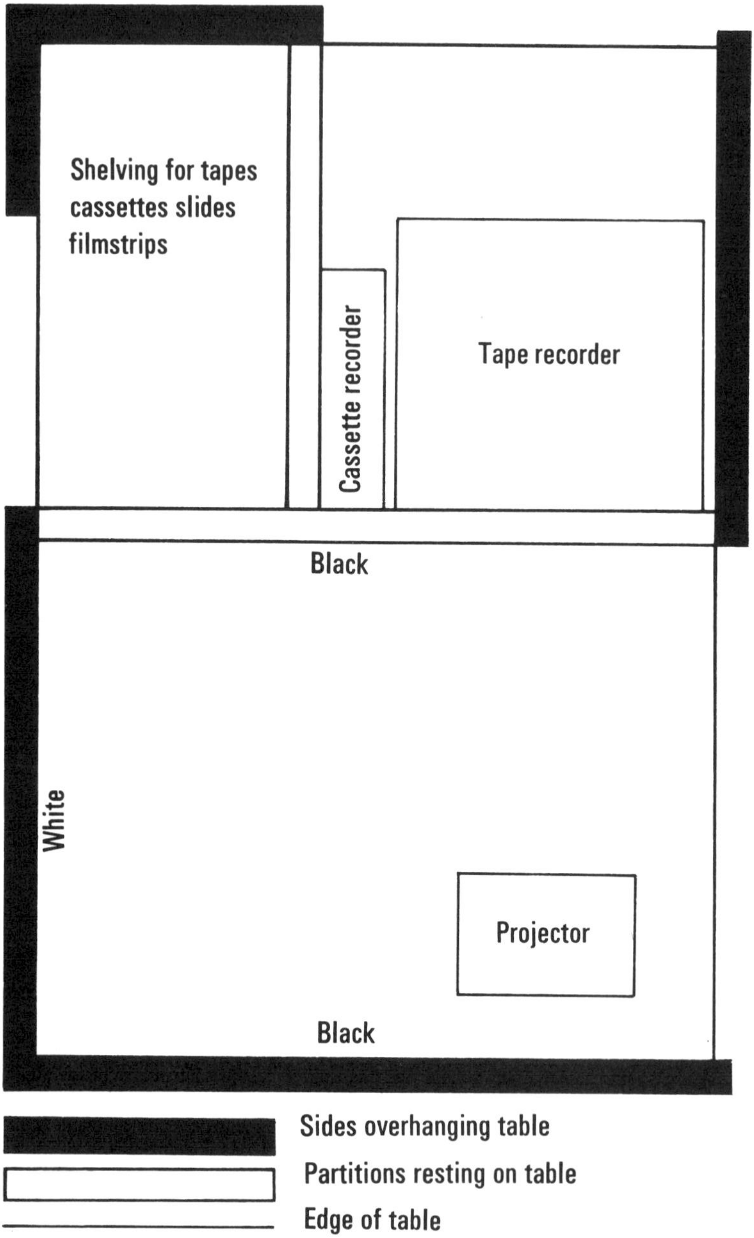

Shelving for tapes
cassettes slides
filmstrips

Cassette recorder

Tape recorder

Black

White

Projector

Black

Sides overhanging table

Partitions resting on table

Edge of table

Fig. 5(a)

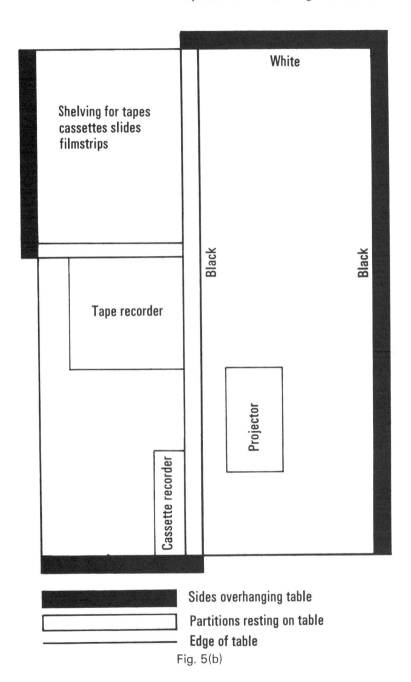

Fig. 5(b)

are accessioned as they arrive. In effect, it is not possible from the numerical sequence to differentiate between media.

2(a) *Separate sequences starting at the same number.* If it has been decided to start the numerical sequence for books at, say, 1001, then all media numerical sequences will start at 1001, but other than those for books each will be prefaced by an indication of the medium to which it refers.

FS1012 will be used for the twelfth filmstrip to be added
CH1012 will be used for the twelfth chart to be added
S1012   will be used for the twelfth slide to be added

If the librarian feels it to be necessary this gives a simple indication of the number of items held in each medium, minus losses and withdrawals. This method requires a separate checklist of accession numbers.

2(b) *Separate sequence using consecutive blocks of numbers.* These blocks will be numerically higher than the anticipated total bookstock. To keep within the limits of a four-figure number for each item, and for the entire stock, approximately a thousand numbers could be allocated to each of three groups of materials. When this expansion is starting it is difficult to visualize how each will develop numerically, but the following suggestions are made:

Illustrations, charts, pictures, etc.   7001–7999
Film, filmstrips, filmloops, slides, etc.   8001–8999
Tapes, records   9001–9999

Of these three groups it is assumed that the fastest-growing will be illustrations and related materials. If 7999 is arrived at unexpectedly quickly it may be possible to double back into the 1001–6999 allocated to books. On the other hand, as items are withdrawn the accession numbers can be used again; while this needs some care, it gives a more realistic figure for stock actually in use. In this re-use of numbers the librarian must remember that he himself must have withdrawn the item which originally bore the number. The number cannot be re-used for a lost item for, as every librarian knows, lost items frequently reappear and so can involve the librarian in much work.

This method also requires a separate checklist of accession numbers.

On balance, it seems that the method first described, of a straight-through sequence, is the easiest to use because, although it does not allow for differentiation, it involves the least time to administer.

CHAPTER SIX

Classification

It is said that those who come to a library do so because they want information or because they want to read imaginative literature; to come within the provision of the modern library the second part of this statement needs some qualification, but it is proposed to leave the division in the broad terms used.

Whether or not the reader has previously organized a school library he will know from his use of the public library that books are broadly placed in one or other of the two groups known as fiction and information books. With the latter it is usual to find a parallel arrangement of books which are too tall to be shelved with the books of normal height, and a further sequence parallel to both available for reference only.

Fiction books

Normally fiction books are conveniently arranged in public and school libraries alphabetically by the author's surname. In some schools where literature is studied to advanced level the stock of books for this purpose is put into the appropriate section of the classification scheme.

ABBOTT / HARRISON

1/9

FIRST VOYAGE OF DISCOVERY 1768-1968

from Notable British Anniversaries. 1968

1/-

SS Great Britain

from Famous British Ships. 1969

Plate 1 Postage stamps

	TAPES	FILMLOOPS FILMSTRIPS SLIDES	CHARTS PICTURES	BOOKS	
	RECORDS				
	● (green)	○ (white)	● (red)	● (black)	
AEROPLANES		S		●	387·7
BADGERS	T	S	CH		599·7
BATS		S	P		599·4
BEES				●	595·79
BLUETITS	R	S	P		598·8
CATHEDRALS		S	P	●	726
CHESS				●	794·1
CHURCHES	T	FS		●	726
CLOUDS		S	P		551·6
COAL MINING			CH	●	622
COSTUME				●	391
COVENTRY CATHEDRAL		S		●	726
DINOSAURS			P	●	568
DRESS				●	391
FOXES		S	P		599·7
HERALDRY		FS		●	929·6
KINGFISHERS	R	FL S			598·89
MUSHROOMS		S			589
MUSICAL INSTRUMENTS	R		CH	●	781·9
OAK TREES		S	P		582·16
OSTRICHES		S	P		598·5
PENGUINS		S	P	●	598·4
POETRY	R			●	821
POND LIFE		S		●	574·92
ROADS	T	FS S		●	388·1
SPACE SHIPS		S		●	387·8
SQUIRRELS		FL S	P		599·3
STAMP COLLECTING				●	769
TREES		S	P	●	582·16
VOLCANOES	T	FS	P	●	551·2

Plate 2

The alphabetical arrangement takes no account of fiction books written around a particular theme, and all school librarians know how often these are asked for. A good example of this problem is historical fiction. Undoubtedly there is a case to be made for putting it with the historical period with which it deals. This may be difficult, however, if the information books are for reference only, since historical fiction would be wanted for borrowing.

It is useful to have lists of books, or authors of books, dealing with particular themes used fictionally. It is not unusual for the public library to provide such lists either as hand-outs in the library or for distribution to schools. If this is not already done there is no harm in asking if such a service could be provided. By indicating the school's holding before putting such a list on the library noticeboard pupils might be encouraged to borrow some of the others from the public library; at the same time such titles might be regarded as suggestions for the librarian and his colleagues to look out for and consider for additions to stock. Normally, as such public library lists relate to their own holding, it would be possible to borrow the books, even one at a time, to have a look at them.

Information books

With the school library needed as an instrument of learning its use is going to be subject-based, so the arrangement of the materials of which it is composed must be by subject.

Less frequently than in the past it occurs to a school librarian that he could produce a classification of the bookstock which would suit his particular school. The shortcomings of an attempt like this are often better appreciated by the librarian who takes over someone else's personal scheme. It may not be a pleasant truth to face, but almost without fail the successor cannot understand what the originator was trying to do; and it has been known for confusion to be confounded and compounded when the successor has had similar pioneering aspirations. Well-intentioned actions can waste valuable time and the librarian would be well-advised to consider – and even surrender to – an established and accepted scheme. In all probability he will disagree with parts of it, but at least it will have stood the test of time and experience. We all make mistakes but we need not repeat those which others have made before us.

It would seem to make sense to use a scheme, even if in a simple form, which the pupils will meet later in a secondary school library, in a library in further education or in their local public library. This gives continuity of experience so that the primary and middle schools can provide a foundation on which the others can build.

In general, public and secondary school libraries use the Dewey Decimal Classification scheme in a full or abridged form; its use in primary and middle schools is therefore helpful both as an introduction to and as a foundation for its more detailed use later. The scheme is unlikely to lose favour; it was adopted for the British National Bibliography in 1950 and it is expected that when a similar production for non-book materials – at present under discussion – finally appears it will be adopted for that also.

A few schools use a more recent scheme, H. E. Bliss's Bibliographic Classification, but although it has some attractive features its main weakness lies in the fact that the pupils who are using it now may never meet it again. This may seem an unfair basis for rejection, but it is not unreasonable for, as already explained, it is important to help pupils to equip themselves for what exists elsewhere. If the principles are grasped at an early stage in education then for those who, for example, go on to university education the change to another scheme, particularly in the older universities, will not present too great a problem. Meanwhile, the majority need meaningful assistance: perhaps it is opportune that the notation of Dewey is a decimal one, making the use of the library part of the pupil's everyday number experience.

Dewey Decimal Classification (DDC)

One of the advantages of DDC lies in the manner in which it can be adapted for use in small or large libraries. One often hears the explanation 'We use a modified Dewey', but this is rather meaningless and misleading because, in its basic form, the scheme is so simple that as the library stock increases the schedules can expand also.

The full schedules of the scheme are published with a separate volume taking the form of a relative subject index.[1] This is used for large libraries and is often used by professional librarians established in secondary schools. For smaller libraries the Abridged Edition should be used; this is now in its 9th edition, published in 1965, and is based on the 17th edition of the full schedules.

In 1961 there appeared an adaptation under the title *Introduction to Dewey decimal classification for British schools,* the second edition of which was published by the School Library Association in 1968. At a time when teachers were beginning to develop libraries in schools this had a calming influence after the teachers' first contact with the full schedules in the local public library; but the choice of the *Introduction . . . for British schools* was often made for the wrong reasons. It may have been because there were not many books in the school, because the pupils in a junior school were not sufficiently familiar with a decimal pattern or because too many pupils in a secondary school did not understand decimalization.

If the *Introduction . . . for British schools* had not been available there almost certainly would have been a plague of personal classification schemes in British school libraries. However, this adaptation, as it stands, raises a number of questions. For example, it is difficult to reconcile the omission of any reference to museums with the part they have played in education since before the publication of the second edition in 1968. Radio engineering appears at 621.384 and television engineering at 621.388, while all insects are classified at 595.7. It would not be unreasonable to expect to find more books in the school library on insects than on radio or television engineering; it would not be unexpected to find a greater percentage of pupils interested in

---

[1] *Dewey decimal classification and relative index.* Forest Press.

beetles (595.76), moths and butterflies (595.78), or ants, wasps
and bees (595.79) than in either radio engineering or television
engineering. If there were still not enough books at 595.7 to
justify an extension one is tempted to question the basis for the
extension given at 621.3 (electrical engineering).

The modern school library is concerned with specific subjects
and the pupils are accustomed to this attitude to information.
The attention given to the content of the various available media
is specific in a way that was not applied to books, so that there is
a growing feeling that the *Introduction . . . for British schools*
has served its purpose. Head teachers of junior and middle
schools which have a central collection of library materials
should ensure that the librarian has a copy of the *Abridged
Dewey decimal classification* (ADC).[1] Although more expensive than the other, it is more useful in present-day situations.

Choosing the Dewey decimal classification in any form does
not imply that it is considered perfect for every school; no
classification scheme would be. Librarians, even more than
teachers, are aware of the restrictions of Dewey, although the
catalogue can help to resolve these to some extent.

It is not the purpose of this chapter to attempt to teach
classification. It is proposed to look at some of the difficulties
teachers have with the scheme itself and with its application. The
ADC has an introduction of some thirty pages which should be
studied; this should be useful particularly to teachers who have
not attended lectures in classification. The School Library
Association can give much help by arranging, through a branch,
a meeting or a 'library workshop' and inviting a professional
librarian to lead it at a simple level for beginners, so that common problems can be discussed to help both teachers and
librarians to understand each other's difficulties. The librarian of
the local public library would almost certainly be willing to meet
local school librarians as a group. It is stressed that this could
advantageously be a mixture of primary and middle school
librarians so that they, too, could benefit from each other's
experiences.

[1] Published by Forest Press.

The plan in brief

The Dewey decimal classification divides all knowledge represented in material form – books, charts, films, filmloops, filmstrips, pictures, records, etc. – into ten classes numbered from 0 to 9. Whereas the classes numbered 1–9 are based on major or related disciplines, Class 0 is used for works dealing with many subjects and for certain disciplines dealing with knowledge in general.

The order of the figures is important: it is 0–9, not 1–9 followed by 0. The pattern of the global 0 dealing with a general approach to a subject, or a total content of a subject, and then 1–9 with its divisions, is worth keeping in mind because it is a recurring pattern.

The notation, which is a translation of the subject word, consists of a three-figure number; no number ever has less than three figures, so that the basic classes 0–9 referred to above appear as numbers 000–900. This initial classification is known as the First Summary and is tabled as follows:

000 Generalities
100 Philosophy and related disciplines
200 Religion
300 The social sciences
400 Language
500 Pure sciences
600 Technology. Applied sciences
700 The arts
800 Literature and rhetoric
900 General geography, history, etc.

Every item added to the library will find a place in one of these classes.

The teacher-librarian in a primary school almost at the first glance will understandably feel that there is not likely to be any probability of having books in Class 100–Philosophy and related disciplines. This foreshadows the fact that in the early stages of the development of a library by no means all the numbers will be in use; these will fill out as the library grows in the primary school, a little more in the middle school, still more in the secondary school, and so on. At the same time there will be many books with the same subject number, e.g. books on trees, churches, castles, etc. Because of the specificity of classification needed for some other media, such as slides, there may not be quite so many spaces by comparison.

Each of the classes shown in the First Summary is divided into ten, thus providing one hundred subject placings known as the Second Summary. Let us take one as an example:

500 Pure sciences
510   Mathematics
520   Astronomy
530   Physics
540   Chemistry
550   Earth sciences
560   Palaeontology
570   Anthropology and biology
580   Botany
590   Zoology

Still dealing with a general approach to a subject, a book about mathematics would be placed at 510; a film about physics at 530; an overhead transparency about astronomy at 520; a general approach to geology in a book at 550. But a book about science in general and containing a little bit about each of these would be classified at the general number 500.

The Third Summary is formed by dividing each division of the Second Summary into ten sections to give a total of one thousand sections, or subject placings; to allow for the future expansion of knowledge not all of these are at present in use. Let us take a division of 510–mathematics:

500 Pure sciences
510   Mathematics
511   Arithmetic
512   Algebra
513   Geometry
514   Trigonometry

515	Descriptive geometry
516	Co-ordinate geometry
517	Calculus
518	
519	Probabilities and statistical mathematics

The basic three-figure number of Dewey has now been reached and this is important in the use of the schedules. Taking the example given above, if a book on trigonometry has been added it will have the number 514; it must not have the number 510. If an overhead transparency gives the diagram and proof of Pythagoras's theorem it will be classified at 513 and not at the general number 510.

A general number must not be used if a specific number is available. Let us assume that someone decides to put all overhead transparencies dealing with mathematical subjects at the general number for mathematics, 510. And let us assume that after a period of time the number of transparencies has grown to forty, all with the number 510; a teacher wants a particular one, say, Pythagoras's theorem, so he may have to look through all forty to find it when at 513 he would perhaps have had to look through only four. It makes a difference for the library user; in the end the librarian will be forced to use a more specific number for each transparency and may have to change the number on all forty.

For further subdivision a decimal point is added to the notation before extending it, and the word 'point' is used when saying the number.

512.07	Five-one-two-point-0-seven	Teaching of algebra
514.9	Five-one-four-point-nine	Problems in trigonometry

Beyond the decimal point the notation never ends with a zero.

There will be times when the librarian will feel that, for primary schools in particular, it might be useful for a variation to be made; there is a distinction between adapting the system and messing around with it so that there is no link with any other library apart from the use of arabic numerals in the notation.

Areas of difficulty

It is not the purpose of this chapter, as has been already mentioned, to deal with the scheme in detail but it may be useful to look at one or two areas of difficulty which arise from time to time.

ADC stresses that there is no one place for a subject *per se*. Subject is subsidiary to discipline.

1. Imagine a book entitled *He gives us our coal* which tells what the miner does from the moment he reports for a shift until he leaves the colliery at the end of it. The index at 'Coals' gives four suggested placings.

(a) 553 – Economic geology: quantitative occurrence and distribution of rocks, minerals, etc.

    550 – Earth sciences   This does not seem right

    500 – Pure science   Not suitable

(b) 338.2 – Primary industries – mineral   Possible

(c) 338.4 – Secondary industries   Possible

    338 – Production   Possible

    330 – Economics. The science that deals with production, distribution, consumption of wealth

                         Doubt is creeping in

    300 – The social sciences. The sciences that deal with social activities and institutions   Not suitable

(d) 622 – Industries – technology

                Mining engineering and operations. Prospecting, surface and underground mining, ancillary equipment and operations, ore dressing, hazards and accidents   This seems to be the placing

In making a decision the librarian, with a choice like this, has to go back through to the discipline.

2. At both 385–387 (Transportation services) and 623–629 (Military, Naval, Aeronautical and other engineering) there are places for ships, railways, aircraft. It may make sense for the librarian, but it may not for the pupils in primary and middle schools, if some books, filmstrips and perhaps a recorded radio

broadcast about boats are placed at 387.2 while others are at 623.82, with a great many items on other subjects not related to them in between. For younger children in particular, the boat is a means of communication between one place and another rather than a product of vehicle engineering. It is suggested that Section 385–387 only be used.

3. The literature class 800 is divided first by language (820–English literature, 840–French literature) and then by form (within 820, 821–Poetry, 822–Drama, 823–Fiction, etc.). Poetry may be collected as the work of an individual poet or as an anthology, i.e. the works of several poets; the usual notation is 821 for individual poets and 821.08 for anthologies. For Byron's poetry, for instance, the notation would be:

821

BYR

Should the librarian feel he would rather avoid the use of a decimal point and figures beyond it he could use 821 for anthologies, and for individual poets put the first three letters of the surname below the figures. For poems by James Reeves the callmark would then be:

821

REE

This callmark on the spine of the book, the cassette container, or the record sleeve, etc., should ensure that poetry by individual poets was arranged on the shelf alphabetically by surname. In the case of anthologies, where only the Dewey number for poetry would be shown, it would be a help to explain to pupils that there are so many names involved they could not be put on the spine of the book.

4. Perhaps interdisciplinary studies will underline the need to do something about the placings of geography and history items about the same country.

Imagine a book on the geography of the United States of America (917.3) and another on the history of the same country

(973). Between these there might be books on South America (918), Australia (919), biography (920) and at 930 the history of the ancient world to c.AD 500. These might be followed by the history of Europe (940), of Asia (950), of Africa (960) and of North America (970) before 973 was reached. This strict use of the Dewey schedules can make life unnecessarily awkward for primary and middle school pupils. If, however, all books, films, tapes, etc., about a country were placed at the history number for that country it would, apart from the increased convenience, make the notation shorter.

5. In using the public library the librarian may already have met different ways of dealing with biographies. In Dewey the general number for biography is 920. For simplicity, some libraries use the letter 'B' instead of 920 and place below this letter the first three letters of the name of the person about whom the biography has been produced:

    B   PURTON, R.W.   David Livingstone
    LIV

Some libraries put at 920 only those biographies which are not clearly related to a specific subject; those which are about people with a strong subject connection are put with the subject, e.g. philosophers (921), scientists (925), engineers (926), musicians (927), etc. (But what does one do with a biography of Leonardo da Vinci?)

   Of this choice it would seem that the simplest solution is that which deals with biography in the way suggested for the classification of the works of individual poets alongside the anthologies, i.e. by putting collective biographies at 920 and, for individual biographies, adding under the 920 the first three letters of the surname of the subject: e.g., for a biography of David Livingstone,

            920
            LIV

6. At the beginning of this chapter mention was made of the treatment of fiction books. One method is to arrange all fiction

alphabetically by the surname of the author, using as the callmark the letter 'F' and adding below it the first three letters of the author's surname to help to bring together on the shelves books by the same author. This is likely to be the best arrangement for primary and middle schools.

When certain books are being studied for examination purposes it is sometimes felt safer to put them into the numerical notation sequence at 823. Here there are two choices. One is to arrange again alphabetically by the surname of the author so that the callmark for a book by Joseph Conrad is

823

CON

The alternative is to adopt a chronological arrangement as is shown in the full Dewey schedules.

7. Until recent years books for children were not usually written about restricted subject areas. For example, books about a number of animals, a group of trees, many birds, and so on, were fairly common but the publication of books specifically about foxes, penguins or other individual animals is more recent. Where the more general classifications were used originally, the tendency was to put the particular with the general.

With the introduction of media other than books into the library the situation has changed, for a slide will not be about insects as a whole, birds as a whole or animals as a whole with classifications of 595.7, 598 and 599 (Mammals) respectively. Instead it is more likely to show a particular insect such as a butterfly (595.78), a particular bird such as a woodpecker (598.7), or a particular mammal such as a monkey (599.8). So the existing classifications will have to be tidied to make the retrieval of the appropriate information quick and simple. As soon as a slide of a butterfly is added, that is the moment to check if there is a book about butterflies at 595.78; if so, it needs to be brought into line.

There are parts of the ADC which do not particularize, however. A slide, filmstrip, or overhead transparency of a particular flower, or a particular tree, might frequently be added to stock, but Dewey in the abridged classification places all flowering plants at 582.13 and all trees at 582.16, leaving the librarian with no alternative but to do likewise with the media. For ease of finding, the most suitable arrangement within these is alphabetically by the common name of the flower or tree.

Whatever problems there are with the classification, the librarian's thoughtful use of the catalogue will often give guidance to the reader.

CHAPTER SEVEN

Cataloguing a Book

As the librarian's means of communicating with his readers is the catalogue it is important that he should be able to identify and understand their problems. Each school librarian will have to decide within his own particular set of circumstances what this will involve, remembering that it is better to simplify, and so help the pupils to help themselves, than to overwhelm them with detail at the outset.

As multi-media resource centres take the place of the traditional book library, primary and middle school librarians will be more concerned than in the past with slow and non-readers. There is a considerable difference between children using public libraries from choice, and therefore motivated to acquaint themselves at least to some extent with library procedures, and those in schools who are expected to use the modern school library as a means of completing curricular assignments.

For a considerable part of each day the teacher-librarian cannot be in the library to give help when and where it is obviously needed; precautions have to be taken to try to stop this gap, and it would seem that this will have to be done mainly through the catalogue. Clarity and consistency are essential in cataloguing, and at each stage in education the library catalogue has to be as simple as the teaching must be if learning is to take place.

The 'language of the catalogue must be the language of the school. It will describe simply what is available so that the great majority of pupils, when they read an entry, will be able to identify their enquiry and be told where to look for what they want. Librarians know that enquirers are not always specific in stating their needs, so cataloguing must at all times be consistent in the type of information that is given and in the order in which it is stated. It is remarkably easy for the occasional omission or change to be interpreted as an absence from the item catalogued or be given some other interpretation which the librarian did not intend.

The catalogue entry should not set a puzzle for the less able, in particular, to solve: when it does, the cataloguing has failed. It may be self-satisfying to provide full cataloguing, but it is certainly naïve to expect those who cannot assimilate to be able to select the information which has relevance for them.

The catalogue is used when someone wants information concerning the contents of the library; when the answer indicates that the material is available a second question naturally follows. 'Is there?' is followed by 'Where is it?' Expanded, the first question will take one of several forms:

1. Is the book by this author and with this title in this library? If so, where shall I look for it?
2. What books are there in this library by this author? If there are any, where shall I look for them?
3. Is there a book in this library with this title? If so, where shall I look for it?
4. What books does the library have on this subject? Where shall I look for them?[1]

In multi-media situations the author is the person, persons or body of people responsible for writing a book, composing music, writing a play or poem, painting a picture, making a recording, etc. To save listing the various media in each case, as has been done here, the word 'author' will tend to be used with this kind of

[1] See Chapter 9, 'The subject index'.

coverage. The questions listed above might be asked about other media.

In school libraries there might be an enquiry in subject form concerning a slide but it is less likely that there will be an enquiry about the photographer who took it. For example, it might be useful to know that the library has a slide showing the Clifton Suspension Bridge; it might be useful, particularly if the school is in or near Bristol, to have an entry under its designer, Isambard Kingdom Brunel; but it is doubtful if there would be any point in having an entry under the name of the person who took the photograph of the bridge, even though his relationship to the photograph is similar to that of an author to the book he writes.

Looking back at these four questions, it is obvious that they centre round three important bibliographic details, namely, author, title and subject; when the presence of the book sought is confirmed, the question common to all concerns the location of the book in the library.

Source of details

All details concerning a book must be taken from the title-page of that book and not from the bookjacket or binding. From the first book by a particular author which is added to stock it is simple enough to accept the author's name as it appears on the title-page; when others follow, however, the catalogue will have to be checked to ensure that there is no variation in the form of name used. If there is any doubt about the two authors being the same, the librarian may be able to check with BNB. There will be title-pages which give all the forenames, others which give some and others which give only initials.

Before starting to catalogue, the librarian should give careful thought to the form which the author's name should take. If he feels it would be best to give all his forenames in full he must realize how much of his time he could spend seeking this information. Can he spare this time? How necessary is it to have forenames at all? Would initials be enough?

Below are two examples of the alphabetical arrangement of entries for nine imaginary books.

Using full forenames

CARVER, Pamela	Going to the museum
CARVER, Patrick	Bees at work
CARVER, Patrick	Dinosaurs
CARVER, Paul John	Postage stamps
CARVER, Paul John	Stamp collecting
CARVER, Paul William	Poems for you
CARVER, Peter	Running and jumping
CARVER, Peter Alexander	Aircraft special
CARVER, Philip	Chess for young people

The alphabetical arrangement is first by author's surname, then by forenames and lastly by title. In the cases of Patrick Carver and Paul John Carver each has two books so, within their respective names, the books are arranged alphabetically by the first word of the title. In alphabetization there is a procedure known as 'nothing before something' which accounts for the entry for Peter Carver coming before that for Peter Alexander Carver; in the former there is nothing following Peter as a forename, while in the latter Peter is followed by Alexander.

Using initials only

CARVER, P.	Bees at work
CARVER, P.	Chess for young people
CARVER, P.	Dinosaurs
CARVER, P.	Going to the museum
CARVER, P.	Running and jumping
CARVER, P. A.	Aircraft special
CARVER, P. J.	Postage stamps
CARVER, P. J.	Stamp collecting
CARVER, P. W.	Poems for you

In arranging the Carver entries alphabetically by the initials of their forenames, and comparing this sequence with the first one,

Books

AP - Art Paints   CH - Charts   P - Pictures
FL - Filmloops   FS - Filmstrips   S - Slides
R - Records   T - Tapes

AEROPLANES	387·7
AEROPLANES	S / 387·7
BADGERS	CH / 599·7
BADGERS	S / 599·7
BADGERS	T / 599·7
BATS	P / 599·4
BATS	S / 599·4
BEES	595·79
BLUETITS	P / 598·8
BLUETITS	S / 598·8
BLUETITS	R / 598·8
CATHEDRALS	726·
CATHEDRALS	P / 726
CATHEDRALS	S / 726
CHESS	794·1
CHURCHES	726
CHURCHES	FS / 726
CHURCHES	T / 726
CLOUDS	P / 551·6
CLOUDS	S / 551·6
COAL MINING	622
COAL MINING	CH / 622
COSTUME	391
COVENTRY CATHEDRAL	726
COVENTRY CATHEDRAL	S / 726
DINOSAURS	568
DINOSAURS	P / 568
DRESS	391
FOXES	P / 599·7
FOXES	S / 599·7
HERALDRY	929·6
HERALDRY	FS / 929·6
KINGFISHERS	FL:S / 598·89
KINGFISHERS	R / 598·89
MUSHROOMS	S / 589
MUSICAL INSTRUMENTS	781·9
MUSICAL INSTRUMENTS	CH / 781·9
MUSICAL INSTRUMENTS	R / 781·9
OAK TREES	P / 582·16
OAK TREES	S / 582·16
OSTRICHES	P / 598·5
OSTRICHES	S / 598·5
PENGUINS	598·4
PENGUINS	P / 598·4
PENGUINS	S / 598·4
POETRY	821
POETRY	R / 821
POND LIFE	574·92
POND LIFE	S / 574·92
ROADS	388·1
ROADS	FS:S / 388·1
ROADS	T / 388·1
SPACE SHIPS	387·8
SPACE SHIPS	S / 387·8
SQUIRRELS	P / 599·3
SQUIRRELS	FL:S / 599·3
STAMP COLLECTING	769
TREES	582·16
TREES	P / 582·16
TREES	S / 582·16
VOLCANOES	551·2
VOLCANOES	P / 551·2
VOLCANOES	FS / 551·2
VOLCANOES	T / 551·2
VOLCANOES : WITH FILMSTRIP	T / 551·2

Plate 3

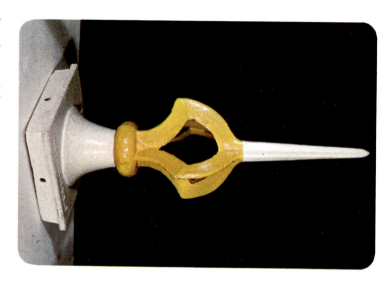

London and South Western
Railway signal finial

Bottle collection

Plate 4

it will be obvious that entries for individual authors are separated because of the first letter of the first word of each title. The librarian will probably be more aware than anyone of the limitations of this system, but on the other hand he will certainly learn that, if he chooses to have full forenames each time, he will have to forego the provision of more necessary and useful services.

Will the pupils be sufficiently conversant with the forenames of authors for the use of initials only to be a deterrent? Will they, or should they, be concerned about the forenames? It is tempting to be knowledgeable but it may be better to be consistent. If the librarian is prepared for the work involved in providing full forenames it may be worth listing each of the above eighteen entries on a card, making the two arrangements as above, and letting several pupils (covering a wide range of abilities) try to find a particular item.

Catalogue cabinets

The traditional catalogue cabinet, which is part of the equipment of public and educational libraries, consists of a drawer or set of drawers standing on a table as shown in Plate 5. Some of these have a stand with legs about 28 in (711 mm) high, and although these are available for two-drawer cabinets the result is a rather insecure piece of furniture for a room as full of lively activity as the modern school library should be.

When the library has its stock catalogued the drawers will contain 5 × 3 in (127 × 76 mm) cards, each of which will give information concerning one book, one slide, one filmstrip or any other single item of information. This accumulation of cards (approximately one thousand in each drawer) will be arranged in a particular order for a specific purpose. One arrangement of cards might consist of all the shelf list cards arranged by their classification number as it appears on the top left-hand corner, so that the order of cards for information books will, in the drawer, be the same as the classified order of the same books on the shelves.

The librarian should not underestimate the size of catalogue cabinet he will require. A single drawer is almost useless because there will be a shelf list card for every copy of every title of a book, and in the same way for every slide, every filmstrip, every chart, etc.

Plate 5   Catalogue cabinets and issue trays

Each card must have a hole near the foot and each catalogue drawer must have a rod which will pass through this hole to keep the cards secure in the drawer and thereby prevent their casual extraction.

If the entries on the cards are to be typed then the cards should be without lines. At the best of times, handwriting is not always easy to read; it presents the less able pupil with problems, and the greater the variety of handwriting the greater the problems for him. Every effort should be made to have the cards typed (see p. 40). If the catalogue cards must be handwritten and if the librarian feels that horizontal lines are necessary it is hoped he will avoid the use of vertical lines as shown in some books on cataloguing procedure. These are distracting and unnecessary for the user; it is therefore the librarian's business to learn the appropriate spacing necessary for drawing attention to the information he provides on the catalogue entry and to make sure that this is passed on to those who prepare the catalogue entries.

Is the book by this author and with this title in the library?

For the enquirer looking for a book by a particular author a card must be provided which gives the surname prominence and includes the title; these are the two facts he knows. When the presence of the card in the catalogue tells the enquirer that the book is in stock then the third item of information – the callmark, or classification number – tells him where the librarian has put it among other books on the same or a related subject.

Let us suppose that the book being sought is by Crabbé and entitled *Boats through the ages*. How has this information been recorded and where has the librarian classified the book?

The classification number is entered on the top left-hand corner of the catalogue card, starting about half an inch (13 mm) from the left edge and from the top. Catalogue cards take harsh treatment from those who use them and, although while in the drawer they should be moved using the fingers of both hands on the sides of the card, most people are lazy and tend to use their finger nails along the tops.

From the start of the classification number, i.e. the 3 of 387, allow ten typing spaces before starting to type the name of the author. In effect this allows for a number like 387.12345, which probably represents a classification of unnecessary detail for primary or middle school pupils; it should allow a space to make the author's name stand out (see Fig. 6).

The author's surname will be in block capitals, followed by a comma and then the initial(s) of his forename(s) and a period. Half an inch (13 mm) under the top line, and starting under the third letter of the author's surname, enter the title of the book beginning with a capital letter. Add the edition if it is other than the first, and add the date.

For ease in consultation these details should be in the top half of the card. It is a simple entry, clearly laid out. Whether the library has one copy or any number of copies of this edition of this title, only one record of it as an author entry is put into the catalogue. This is different from the shelf list card which has one card for each separate copy of a title.

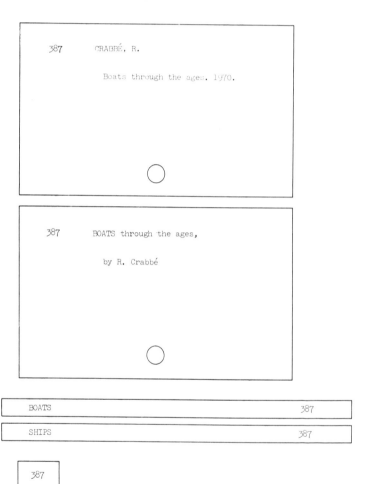

Fig. 6

The classification number always appears in the same position, and to prevent confusion the accession number should never be on the front of a catalogue card, but should be put on the reverse (see Fig. 9, p. 85).

The card takes its place in an alphabetical sequence of author cards with its position determined by the name in block capitals. This sequence is known as the author index. It is constructed solely to guide the reader quickly to what he seeks. It does not give details which describe the book: for example, it does not give the place of publication or the publisher's name which form part of the imprint of the book. It gives no information on the collation such as the number of pages of introduction, the number of pages of text, the kinds and numbers of illustrative material, the height of the book, or the series.

As far as the primary or middle school pupil is concerned these omitted details are probably not necessary; in general terms their inclusion would be more likely to deter than to encourage use of the catalogue. At this stage this is an important consideration. For those who want more details the book itself or else the shelf list card will supply them.

In answering the question posed, the card, through the information on it, is saying that there is in this library a book by Crabbé – in fact by R. Crabbé – with the title *Boats through the ages*; it was published in 1970 and it will be found among the information books in the numerical sequence with the number 387 at the foot of the spine.

The librarian's cataloguing has to be clear-cut and definite: if the book is in the library and the enquirer knows the name of the author there will be a card in the author index, but if there is no card then there is no book by that author and with that title. Whenever the book is withdrawn this card and all entries relating to the book must be withdrawn.

What books are there in this library by this author?

The author index brings together all books by an author, so it also answers the second question.

Is there a book in this library with this title?

For the enquirer knowing only the title and probably having no idea of the author's name a card must be provided giving prominence to the title and including the author's name. Although the enquirer may not be interested in the name of the author, it should be given; the linking of the two pieces of information singles out a specific book and gives additional information about it.

On this question of title entries in the catalogue it would be natural for the librarian to consider the provision made in the public library; if he cannot recall what is done there it is probably because there are no title entries. Before he makes a decision to follow this practice, however, it might be helpful to compare the two situations, for circumstances do influence each area of librarianship.

The provision of a title entry for every book in the public library would almost double the size of the catalogue and greatly increase the use of staff time in doing so. While it is no substitute for title entries, the fact remains that public library staff could give a verbal answer to most such enquiries. In addition they would have access to catalogues and bibliographies which would provide the answers. Where the primary or middle school library is concerned it is usually not within the librarian's financial resources to provide catalogues and bibliographies.

Some school librarians contend that there is no need for an entry under the title of an information book since the book can be found by using the subject index. This makes two assumptions. Firstly, it assumes that the pupil knows that the book of which he knows the title has been judged by the librarian to be an information book. Secondly, it assumes that the pupil knows what the librarian thinks is the subject of the book. Not only are these considerable assumptions as they stand, but they are not easy to accept on behalf of pupils with a wide range of chronological, reading and ability ages. Moreover, most librarians know the problems involved in classifying historical fiction and animal stories.

What is needed is a return to the situation where the information in the pupil's possession is used to give him the opportunity of finding the answer for himself. The teacher teaches, or makes it possible for the pupil to learn and to practise, skills which have been demonstrated – how to find a book, for example, with certain pieces of information concerning it.

In this case the enquirer knows that the title of the book is *Boats through the ages.* How will the librarian have prepared a title entry card?

As in the case of the author entry, the classification number appears on the top left corner of the card, starting about half an inch (13 mm) from the left-hand edge and the same from the top. From the start of the classification number allow ten typing spaces, then in block capitals type the first word of the title, i.e. BOATS. This word on this card is in the same position as the author's surname on the other, which makes it easy on the eye when looking through a number of cards in a drawer of the catalogue cabinet: the capitalization in both cases makes this first word stand out to attract attention. The remainder of the title will be in lower case letters and, after the last word, a comma.

Half an inch (13 mm) under this line and starting under the third letter of the first word of the title type the word 'by', followed by the author's initial and lastly his surname (see Fig. 6).

In neither entry has any reference been made to the existence of illustrations. There is a body of opinion that believes it can be understood that if the text warrants them the publisher will have ensured that illustrations are included; and as far as books for children are concerned, illustrations are essential and their inclusion can be assumed.

Figure 7 shows a title entry for a book without an author and this one includes a broad statement of illustrative material contained in the book. Against the omission in the previous example the librarian might weigh the inclusion in this: the omission makes the pupil handle the book for himself to discover the make-up of the book and later, in his subsequent report in writing or on tape concerning his assignment, he can use the knowledge he has acquired from his own discovery.

Public librarianship tends to provide a personal service to library users, to look for and produce an answer when an enquiry is made; no one would quarrel with that. Inherent in the purpose of educational librarianship is an important teaching role; if learning to use a library is a basic skill then this approach requires particular emphasis. Detailed cataloguing will be necessary in higher education, but the primary or middle school librarian has to be realistic in trying to develop confidence in the use of the library.

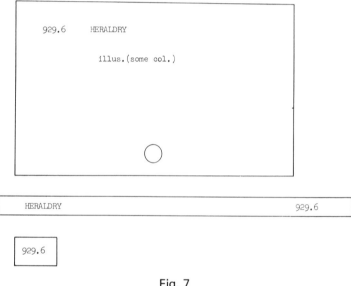

Fig. 7

Alphabetical arrangement of catalogue cards

When author and title entries have been provided for all the books in the library the cards will be brought together into one alphabetical sequence, so that the three examples just given will be filed under 'Boats', 'Crabbé' and 'Heraldry'. There is no more need to provide two separate sequences for authors and titles than there is to divide a dictionary so that one section contains nouns and adjectives, another verbs and adverbs and a third what is left over. Training in the use of a catalogue complements training in the use of a dictionary.

The librarian should try to guard against the possibility of the pupil misfiring when he tackles the catalogue. The pupil trying to find *Black Beauty* may be put off by the fact that Mary Black lives next door and that for her 'Black' is a surname. To try to help, some school librarians use coloured catalogue cards; if white is used for author entries then another colour is used for title entries. Catalogue cards vary in thickness according to their quality and this causes a tactual difficulty which can be awkward. It may be convenient to buy ordinary white catalogue cards from a nearby stationer, but coloured cards must be ordered from a supplier of library stationery. Unless he has cards of the same quality, the manipulation of the cards, as they are mixed, can be irritating. Either always deal with the same library stationer or else send a sample of the card which is normally used when ordering.

CHAPTER EIGHT

Cataloguing Materials other than Books

As they view the change in the content of the library many school librarians feel that they have only just become accustomed to the details required for cataloguing books when a whole range of unfamiliar terms presents itself.

What will be recorded and how will it be done? How much will be recorded for the benefit of the librarian and his colleagues and how much do the pupils require? Teachers may need to know that a filmloop runs for 2 min 35 sec. It is less certain that a pupil will require this information. If all transparencies are made to fit the one projector available, does the size have to be given?

However, among pupils an interesting development is taking place which could influence the librarian's decision. The fluent reader will assimilate a good deal of information from a catalogue card entry, while the slow reader will be considerably less responsive. Non-book materials make a greater impact than the book on the slow and non-reader; such pupils tend to be more interested in the practical and technical sides of these materials, yet, as a result of this kind of experience, they are beginning to show more interest in books in order to satisfy the curiosity aroused.

MEDIUM									
CLASSN. NO.									
(ACCESSN. NO.)									
AUTHOR									
TITLE									
PUBLISHER/PRODUCER/DISTRIBUTOR									
DATE									**ORDER**

CH	**CHART**			hx	w mm	b/w col.	
P	**ILLUSTRATION**			hx	w mm	b/w col.	
P	**PRINT**			hx	w mm	b/w col.	
F	**FILM**	16mm 8mm super 8mm si. sd.		min sec	b/w col.		
FL	**FILMLOOP**	8mm super 8mm		min sec	b/w col.		
FS	**FILMSTRIP**		sf. df. frs.	b/w col.			
S	**SLIDE**			slides b/w col.			
R	**RECORD**	mono 33.3rpm 7ins 10ins 12ins / stereo 45rpm 178mm 254mm 305mm sides					
T	**TAPE**	reel ins $1\frac{7}{8}$ips $3\frac{3}{4}$ips $7\frac{1}{2}$ips / mm mono / cassette stereo 48mmps 95mmps 190mmps		min sec			

NOTES	SERIES	NO.
ADDED ENTRIES	1. subject	
	2. composer/author	
	3. performer/narrator	
	4. series	
TRACINGS	1. subject	
	2. composer/author/ performer/narrator	
	3. series	
STANDARD BOOK NUMBER	ADDED TO STOCK / /197	

Fig. 8

ABBREVIATIONS

b/w	black and white		**mono**	monaural
cm	centimetres		**nd**	no date
col	coloured		**rpm**	revolutions per minute
df	double frame		**s**	side
frs	frames		**sd**	sound
h	height		**sec**	seconds
ins	inches		**sf**	single frame
ips	inches per second		**si**	silent
mm	millimetres		**stereo**	stereophonic
min	minutes		**w**	width

This situation must be evaluated in each school and will depend on the progress made so far with library skills. Although it may be decided to be sparing with details on the catalogue cards themselves, there must still be a full record of them made as each item is received into stock.

A pro-forma for non-book materials

Many librarians, the author included, have worked with pro-formas in cataloguing. It is costly to use the librarian as a typist: when clerical assistance is available, help must be given with the kind of information required and the order in which it is recorded together with guidance in the standardization of abbreviations. It may be that the librarian already keeps a standard list of abbreviations for publishers, to avoid mixtures like O.U.P., OUP, Oxford U.P., Oxford Univ. P., Ox. Un. Pr., or Oxford, for Oxford University Press.

The pro-forma shown in Fig. 8 lists the kinds of media most likely to be found in primary and middle school libraries. For those schools with others like models, artefacts, specimens, games, video tapes, etc., a space has been left in which the librarian can insert appropriate details, taking guidance from the media already there.

On receiving material, the librarian will link the pro-forma with the shelf list card (see Fig. 1, p. 20), which will be completed from details subsequently added to the pro-forma.

The medium will be indicated in full in block capitals as it appears lower down the pro-forma and as it will be copied onto the catalogue entry. On the catalogue card it will be typed over the classification number to form with it the call number; to keep the catalogue cards to the minimum amount of detail the medium need not again be stated. As in the author and title main entries (Figs 6 and 7), the classification number will be on the same level as the author's name or the title, respectively. In the case of non-book materials the name of the medium will be typed two spaces above the classification number and will start immediately above the first figure of that number, for example:

```
FILMSTRIP
598.4    PENGUINS in their rookeries and

          at the zoo.
```

(Note that the second line of the title is indented to start under the third letter of the first word of the title so that the latter stands out for easy recognition in the catalogue drawer.)

The accession number in a book is not normally visible because it appears behind the title-page; although it appears there with the classification number, it is only the latter which is shown on the spine of the book. By their nature, non-book media, as opposed to the record of them, need a different treatment and one way of identifying a particular slide or filmstrip is to incorporate the accession number, in brackets (to avoid confusion with the classification number), into the call number. Figures 10 (p. 87) and 12 (p. 89) show this applied to a filmstrip container and a slide.

At this stage it may be necessary to indicate on the pro-forma what medium is being recorded. This can be done by circling the appropriate item, ticking through it or underlining it, as the librarian chooses; any of these is simpler than deleting the alternatives. There will also be figures to be inserted in appropriate places.

Charts, illustrations and prints

Charts, illustrations and prints require a statement of dimensions and an indication as to whether they are in black and white or in colour. Dimensions are always given in the order height by width, and as this is in alphabetical order it should be easily remembered. At this stage in the advance towards metrication it is not clear which unit of measurement will be used for different items. The Imperial measure is given because this still has more meaning for many people than the metric equivalent which is given in brackets, using the millimetre. Should the centimetre emerge supreme then a decimal point between the last two figures will give the measurement in centimetres.

A chart entitled 'Song birds' shows 57 birds in colour. It is published by Educational Productions Ltd, measures 27 × 40 in (698 × 1016 mm), has the accession number 1230 and is classified at 598.2. These details will all be entered on the pro-forma with the word 'CHART' circled, ticked or underlined. It is doubtful if a useful purpose will be served by including the name of the publisher on the catalogue card. The accession number will appear on the reverse side of the catalogue card. On the chart itself, and on the container of the chart if there is one, the accession number will appear in brackets as part of the call number.

If it is likely that some of the birds shown on such a chart can be seen locally, the librarian may want to make a further record by inserting, in the section 'TRACINGS 1. subject', simply '57 birds'; when the catalogue card is typed this can remain (on the reverse) as 'Tr. 57 birds'. This is one of those exceptional cases which crop up now and again; as far as book cataloguing is concerned it may be without parallel in the library, but it demonstrates the need for adaptable methods of information retrieval.

Figure 9 shows the title card as it would be typed from the pro-forma, and shows the reverse of the card, upside down, with the accession number and the tracings stated numerically, but not listed.

The use of a strip index in place of a card index is explained in Chapter 9. Figure 9 shows subject entry strips for three of the birds illustrated on the chart. The ADC number for birds in general is 598.2, which would be used when a book, filmstrip, etc., deals with more than one type of bird. If there already is a book, slide or filmstrip on, say, blackbirds, the ADC number will be 598.8; something on cuckoos will have the number 598.7. (Subject index words always take the plural form even when there is, for instance, only one blackbird on the slide.) These entries, on the appropriate coloured strip or with a coloured stick-on to indicate a chart, will show the classification number for the chart (598.2) because to find the illustration the chart must be found first.

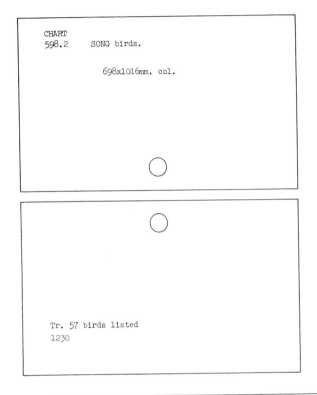

```
CHART
598.2      SONG birds.

                698x1016mm. col.
```

```
              Tr. 57 birds listed
              1230
```

BLACKBIRDS	598.2
CUCKOOS	598.2
NIGHTINGALES	598.2

```
CHART
598.2
(1230)
```

Fig. 9

Films, filmloops, filmstrips and slides

In the second part of the pro-forma – dealing with films, filmloops, filmstrips and slides – it can be seen that details have to be considered which, in general, did not apply to the media in the first group. The last choice shown, between black and white and colour, might warrant additional consideration for noting in the callmark because of the nature of the media.

Consider a filmstrip entitled *Daily life in Verulamium*, with L. B. Gribbin named as the producer. When this filmstrip was made in 1964 there was little being done to align this kind of medium with the book; it is probably safe to state that the word 'author' would not have been contemplated even if the notes were written by L. B. Gribbin. As one would understand that a book was published by a publisher, so one would see that, similarly, the filmstrip was published by the Educational Foundation for Visual Aids. Although L. B. Gribbin's name would be inserted as the 'author' (not as the producer), his name is unlikely to be used by the pupils and, as with most non-book materials, it is the title which will be circled as the main entry. The title is entered as it appears on the title-frame of the filmstrip.

Not every filmstrip shows a date. This one does and the date 1964 is inserted. If there is no date on the filmstrip itself but it appears on the notes or elsewhere, it will be inserted in brackets, e.g. (1964). The number of frames will be inserted and that part circled. It is a coloured filmstrip so there will be a.circle round 'col'.

The librarian should devise clear labelling which will discourage any unnecessary handling of film in its various forms. Once the pupil has found the subject in which he is interested he may have forgotten certain details of the catalogue entries; in fact he may not have used the catalogue but only the subject index. The label which is put on the container will state the medium, the classification number, and the accession number in brackets. The word or contraction which the librarian will choose to describe all the filmstrips may be 'FILMSTRIP' if the label is wide enough; it may be 'F'STRIP'; or it may be simply 'FS'. At that part of the call number on the label there could be an indication if it is in colour – no indication for black and white would be necessary. Figure 10 shows a label for the top of a filmstrip container with the letter 'C', for 'colour', inserted after the contraction used for a filmstrip. The librarian will want to guard against a superfluity of symbols and contractions, but this one seems unobtrusive and useful.

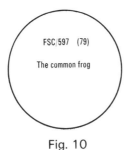

FSC/597 (79)

The common frog

Fig. 10

When dealing with filmloops the information transferred from the pro-forma will depend on the machine or machines available in the school. Although the section 'Super 8 mm' will be ringed, ticked or underlined on the pro-forma, it will be necessary to give this information on the catalogue entry only if there is an 8 mm projector available as well as a Super 8 mm projector. Again, a statement on the label about colour would be unnecessary if all the filmloops were in colour. One cannot stress too often that unnecessary symbols and contractions should be omitted.

Figure 11 shows the entry for a filmloop, the strip for the subject index, a label for the filmloop cassette and another for the cassette container.

Slides are single units in themselves but they can also be combined to make a slideset: when this happens, at the part marked 'SLIDE' add 'SET' to give 'SLIDESET', which would be the medium to be inserted on the top line of the pro-forma.

A slideset might be listed as 'Animals – Scotland' and contain twelve slides in colour. Of the twelve, two might be worth listing separately because they are often mentioned. If the librarian inserts a word to explain, for instance, the dash between the two

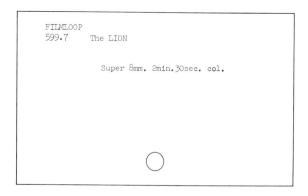

```
FILMLOOP
599.7    The LION

              Super 8mm. 2min.30sec. col.
```

```
    LIONS                                              599.7
```

```
FLC
599.7
(1266)
```

Fig. 11

words in the title suggested, then it will be enclosed in brackets. Figure 12 shows the title entry for the slideset, three entries for the subject index which will be listed on the reverse of this card, one label for the slideset container and three examples of the stick-on for each of three slides. In this case the contraction 'SS' has been used for slideset; this will direct the slide to the slideset if it becomes separated from it.

Aural materials

Aural materials require a different set of descriptive 'words'. While some of the necessary information will appear on a record there can easily be omissions or statements which are difficult to trace both on records and on tape. The librarian may feel that more is needed than a simple statement on a catalogue card which in any case may not have been seen.

A stereo recording must not be played on a mono player un-

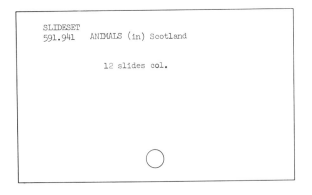

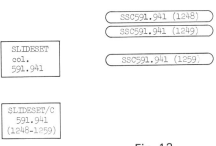

Fig. 12

less a suitably wired stereo pick-up is used: otherwise considerable damage will be done. If there is a possibility of hasty
enthusiasm taking over from careful checking when there are
two types of machine, the librarian is advised to put a notice in
large letters on each, stating the type of record it takes; the centre of each record should carry a coloured sticker stating
whether it is mono or stereo, even if this fact is stated on the
record and even when the catalogue entry is specific about it.

Important also is the speed at which the record should be played. Those accustomed to playing records know that, normally, the 7 in (177 mm) record is played at 45 rpm and the 12 in (305 mm) at 33.3 rpm. As well as there being some users who are not accustomed to records, there may be in the library foreign records which do not conform to these standards. The librarian may feel that these items should be included in the catalogue entry and, therefore, that standardization would be helpful. Even if there is uncertainty about the wisdom or need for details to be given on entries for other media, aural media, records in particular, should be considered as a special case. So much damage can be done to a record through misuse that repetition of information may not come amiss.

Figure 13 shows a main entry under the title of a recording of a poetry anthology. A glance at the pro-forma indicates that the first statement to be circled is mono or stereo; from this the reader is told the kind of machine he requires. Next comes the speed at which it should be played; most typewriters will have to type decimals rather than fractions, so in this case it is 33.3 rpm. For handwritten entries on the shelf list card the normal fraction would be used. Thirdly comes the diameter of the record which, on the entry, has been given in inches and in millimetres. Lastly comes a statement about the sides used.

This kind of record and some music records contain a great deal of information, probably not all of which need be recorded on the catalogue entry or on the shelf list card. If the pro-formas are retained the librarian may consider it useful there. Obviously an anthology consists of a number of poems. When the anthology is in book form, poems can be traced, or else known to be excluded, by consulting the book itself. Tracking down a poem can sometimes be a long and tedious job without the help of Granger's *Index to poetry*,[1] and there are so many references to anthologies in that work that the task of location within one's own library stock can be a monumental exercise.

Every effort should be made to minimize the handling of

[1] Published by Columbia University Press. The librarian should make himself familiar with this work, as well as with Helen Morris's *Where's that poem?* (Blackwell).

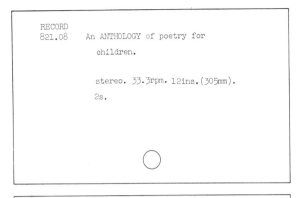

```
    RECORD
    821.08    An ANTHOLOGY of poetry for
                 children.

                 stereo. 33.3rpm. 12ins.(305mm).
                 2s.
```

```
    RECORD
    821.08    JOHN Gilpin, by W. Cowper.  In An
                 anthology of poetry for
                 children.

                 stereo. 33.3rpm. 12ins.(305mm).
                 s.2 band 5.
```

```
    POETRY  Anthologies                              821.08
```

```
    RECORD
    821.08
    (1232)
```

Fig. 13

records. In this particular anthology not all the poems would be wanted, but for those which might it would be worth making an entry in the catalogue, with the appropriate reminders in the shelf list card, on the reverse of the main entry if there is no shelf list, or on the pro-forma if this is retained for use as an accessions record.

One of the poems in this anthology is the well-known 'John Gilpin'. The layout of an analytical entry is shown in Fig. 13.

The first word of the name of the poem is shown in block capitals to make it stand out, and the title is followed by the name of the poet in the manner shown. The reader now has to be directed to the anthology so, following on with the introductory word 'In', underlined as shown, state its title, starting with a capital letter but without further capitalization because there is no filing involved: complete the information given in the main entry. Four spaces below this last line, add the side and the band.

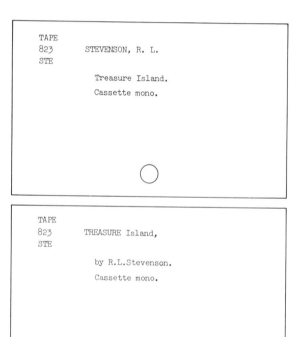

Fig. 14

Another way of making an analytical entry is to make a second main entry card exactly like the first in spacing and layout. The title of the poem sought is known; its exact location has to be given, so, in that order, both items will be indicated on the card. Pupils and staff will have been told that cards in a catalogue are filed alphabetically by the first word in block capitals other than the name of the medium; the first word of the title of the poem will be in block capitals.

Starting two spaces above the title of the record, the title of the poem should be in line with the name of the medium. In this case, start above the space between 'An' and 'anthology', i.e. the third typing space from the beginning of the heading, to start like this:

```
RECORD      JOHN Gilpin, by W. Cowper. In
821.08      An ANTHOLOGY of poetry for

            children.
```

Under 'stereo, etc.' add s.2 band 5.

The second example gives an impression of crowding additional information on an existing set of details; this is the method used by large libraries which use duplicate copies of the main entry either made by a duplicating process or bought from the BNB. In the case of the BNB card the typeface is small with the result that there is less crowding. On the other hand, the first example looks more like an entry on its own.

For analytical entries such as this the librarian should consult his colleagues about which poems are likely to be wanted; while he will be guided by their needs, he will be more aware than they of the demands which are made as a whole in this field. As soon as an enquiry is made about a poem, for example, or as soon as the librarian knows that one has been used, an entry could be put into the catalogue; if it has been played or read to the pupils it is possible that someone will want it again.

Recorded stories are catalogued with the main entry under the author of the book and an entry under the title. Figure 14 shows an entry similar to Fig. 6. In this entry two forms of the callmark are used to show that when the library has only one size of self-adhesive label and it takes three lines only of typing, the form 823/STE can be used; in the same way, F/STE can be used if this is the form the librarian has chosen.

For entries of musical works the possessive form of the composer's name as the first word of the title obviates the search for and the knowledge of forenames which vary in the less dependable reference works (see Fig. 15). Where the school's collection is a large one which may have to cater for various members

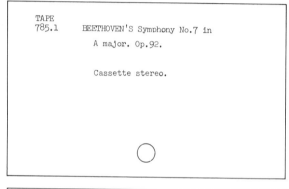

SYMPHONIES   785.1

TAPE
785.1
(1247)

Fig. 15

of the Bach family, there will almost certainly be a professional librarian on the staff; the pursuit of bibliographic details is a major part of his expertise and he will have ensured that he has the tools of his trade at hand.

This is a short entry to avoid overwhelming the average pupil with details: those pupils and colleagues who want more information will find it on the pro-forma or on the shelf list card and, of course, on the cassette if it is not on loan. The library is for all pupils and in providing a catalogue the librarian is, basically, providing a finding tool. Too much detail will deter.

CHAPTER NINE

The Subject Index

The teacher-librarian knows that where the library is a teaching-learning tool the approach of the pupils is largely subject-based. 'What does the library have on this subject and where shall I find it?' Two simple questions need two simple answers which state the subject asked for and the callmark given by the librarian.

When the librarian considers the book for classification he has the shelf list card (Fig. 1, p. 20) beside him. Let us assume that the book is about pottery, for which the ADC number is 738.1. This number is put in the appropriate section in the top left corner of the card. The librarian now has to decide the word which describes the subject in a language which his pupils understand. 'Pottery' describes this and it seems unnecessary to fuss around with an expression like 'ceramic arts'. In the section marked 'Requested by' on the shelf list card the entry for the subject index can be shown as 's.i. – Pottery'. From these two items the subject entry will be made for the kind of index decided by the librarian.

While there is no single method which has to be used it is important that the subject index be simply constructed to meet the needs and capabilities of those who will use it. It will be flexible in construction to permit the insertion of new entries so that a strict alphabetical sequence is maintained. Entries should not be made in pages of a notebook because, although these can initially be spaced in alphabetical order, as additions are made spaces are seldom used as planned, with the result that inevitably it grows untidily and becomes difficult to use.

At the outset it is often felt that there will not be many entries needed, but as its usefulness is appreciated it grows; it is this growth which the librarian must try to envisage, if for no other reason than to avoid having to change the method adopted and start again with a new type of index.

With the structuring of courses and assignments for individual learning much more attention will have to be paid to indexing than has been customary with books. Visual material in the form of slides is an example; it is not unusual for three, four or more suggestions for subject indexing to result from giving one slide to half-a-dozen colleagues for scrutiny.

Some writing on the indexing of slides has bordered on the hysterical, almost as if the British Museum catalogue were required in every school library. The school librarian is concerned with the real and expectant needs of the pupils in his school. While it would be overwhelming and quite unnecessary for the librarian to index every car or every church on each slide, picture or book in stock, the apparently ordinary church might be the only one giving the reader the opportunity to see quarter-boys on the church tower.

Some librarians prefer to wait until a search has to be made for something before inserting a covering entry in the subject index, but this would appear to be contrary to the purpose of the 'resource centre'. It would be better to find a few colleagues willing to examine slides, filmstrips, and tapes, for example, to let them offer suggestions from which the librarian could select if necessary.

Let us look at three methods of constructing a subject index, one using catalogue cards and two being forms of displayed or 'visual' index. All are in use and are proving helpful to pupils.

Index on catalogue cards
This is the traditional method most likely to be found in public

libraries. It is an alphabetical sequence of catalogue cards, each of which gives only two items of information, namely, the subject word and, in the case of the Dewey Decimal Classification, the subject number. An example of such a card is shown in Fig. 16, with the subject word clearly in block capitals on the left and the notation on the right.

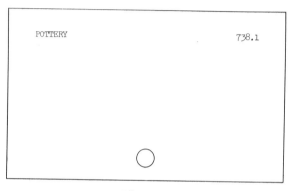

Fig. 16

The reader has come with his subject query and he has been told the location of this subject in the arrangement of books. If the book or books with this number have been borrowed, the pupil's ability to pursue his subject back through the classification will depend to some extent on the librarian's guidance.

While some instruction in the use of the catalogue can be given to a class or group of pupils, the most effective instruction is given individually as queries arise. The temptation facing librarians is to find the answer for the enquirer; until the pupil begins to gain confidence, the librarian should work through the process with him. In the example shown in Fig. 16 he will talk his way from 738.1 to the index of anything at 738, to 730, 700 and to the index of an encyclopaedia if there is one in the library. Referring to the subject word as it appears in the text of an encyclopaedia may not produce the information required; every good encyclopaedia has an index which should always be used to cover aspects of the subject in related material.

Visual indexes

Using the basic principle of subject word and subject number for information material, changes have been rung for simplification and ease in consultation. Catalogue card manipulation is known to be uninviting and many users of libraries feel it is the kind of experience they are prepared to forego; proof is in the number who, while knowing what they seek, prefer to spend more time searching the shelves in the hope of coming across suitable material. The term 'visual index' may, strictly, seem a strange description but it is used to stress that the index is there to be seen rather than having to be looked for in a drawer.

Pegboard index (made by hand)

Figure 17 shows a drawing of a pegboard subject index as it is

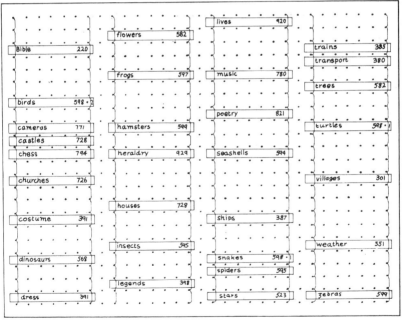

Fig. 17

being built up; it represents a sheet of pegboard 32 × 24 in (813 × 610 mm) with the holes one inch (25 mm) apart. Strips showing the subject word with its corresponding subject number can be spaced in columns alphabetically and held behind double lines of elastic threading.

This type of index can be fitted to a wall above a bookcase, although care must be taken to ensure that the board is not too high for the entries to be read easily; a narrower version can be attached to the ends of back-to-back projecting bookcases where, with the need for power points on walls and the proximity of the necessary machines for listening and viewing, bookcases may have been moved from their former back-to-the-wall siting.

The more useful the subject index becomes the greater the enthusiasm generated and therefore the faster the expansion of the number of entries and, accordingly, the space required. It is there as part of the library environment for every pupil who enters; it invites participation and acts as a stimulus to the pupil's daily reading and number experience. One of the interesting results is the speed with which so many pupils begin to absorb the classification numbers for subjects in which they are interested and how, with their newly found confidence, they begin to help those still finding their way. This is the kind of assimilation which tends to take by surprise the librarian who is going through the stage when he feels he always has to consult the Dewey schedules and will never be independent.

Construction. A side-on view of the pegboard shows how the elastic threading is done (Fig. 18). Taking a piece of elastic thread at least twice as long as the height of the pegboard, in this case 55–60 in (1400–1525 mm) long, thread it from the back of the pegboard through the top left-hand hole, to the front; bring it back through the second top hole of the same column, forward through the third, back through the fourth, and so on, following the direction of the dotted line in the illustration. When the lowest hole has been reached work back up to the top again, as shown by the firmer line. Before fastening the ends securely at the back and out of sight, the elastic thread will have to be tightened sufficiently to prevent its sagging.

Starting at the seventh hole from the left in the top row, repeat this process. It should now be possible to pass behind two loops in the same row, i.e. on the same level, a piece of card $7\frac{3}{4} \times \frac{7}{8}$ in (196 × 22 mm) to leave the card projecting $\frac{7}{8}$ in (22 mm) beyond each side of the elastic thread (see Fig. 17). Where this is the desired overlap, the third line of elastic threading will then be started at the ninth column of holes and separated from the second threading by a column of unused holes. The fourth threading will be six holes distant from the third.

Fig. 18

As can be seen in Fig. 17, when two cards are adjacent they should almost meet over the line of holes separating those lines of elastic thread which are close together. If it is considered unnecessary to have such a big overlap to ensure that the cards will not slip out, then the spacing of the threading will change. Instead the columns of elastic threading could use the first and seventh, eighth and fourteenth, fifteenth and twenty-first lines of holes. The length of the subject card would then be $6\frac{3}{4}$ in (171 mm) to leave a projection of approximately $\frac{3}{8}$ in (9 mm) beyond the elastic thread on each side of the card. The width of the pegboard will be altered to suit the threading plan.

For good wear the cards for the subject entries should be strong; sometimes they are covered with Takibak (see p. 30) to keep them clean. They can be cut ready for use and completed as books, slides, pictures, etc., are added to stock. As the subject word should start immediately to the right of the left-hand elastic thread and the subject number should finish immediately to the left of the right-hand elastic thread, a space of six inches (152 mm) is available (see Fig. 19).

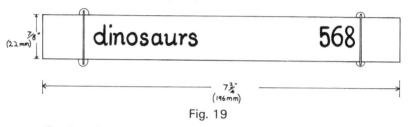

Fig. 19

On the whole a simple three-figure Dewey classification notation has been used because this kind of strip index would be used with young children. There may be occasions when it will be convenient to classify beyond the decimal point and it will do no harm to introduce the decimal point in a small way. In the Abridged Decimal Classification Dewey places reptiles at 598.1 and birds at 598.2; as both are likely to be represented it seems better to separate them in this way than to keep them both at 598 where they tend to look a little incongruous. In Fig. 17 the figure after the decimal point has been put beyond the elastic thread; the individual librarian can decide whether this is useful or unnecessary.

The index is likely to grow rapidly, particularly when synonyms have to be included. Do not refer from one word to a synonym; if the pupils use both 'verse' and 'poetry' then make an entry for each and on each give a direction to 821.

The full board should be used from the outset, with the early part of the alphabet occupying the top left corner and the end occupying the lower right. Care must be taken to ensure that the strips relate to actual material in the library. Before removing a card because, for example, a picture on that subject has been withdrawn, the librarian should check to make sure that nothing on the same subject is present in another medium.

When the number of entries becomes considerable there is a temptation to use pegboard with a smaller spacing of holes, but the index may be ignored if the necessarily narrower card dictates smaller writing which cannot easily be read.

Some junior schools have effectively combined this form of subject index with the colour-coded subject groupings of books in central collections in infant departments on the same site. Books in infant schools are normally displayed with their colourful fronts showing and when there is a central, freely accessible collection like this some kind of broad subject grouping is helpful for the children. Colours can be used to identify subject groups. When groupings and colours have been agreed, the appropriate coloured stickers can be fixed to the top right corner of the front cover of each book and to the front edge of the corresponding shelf or strut. Only colour should be used as a differentiating symbol at this stage; to introduce shape as well might be confusing. Here is one suggested grouping of subjects with the ADC main classes shown in brackets:

Bible stories	white	(200)
Transport	yellow	(300)
Science	green	(500 and 600)
Poetry and dictionaries	red	(800)
Countries and people	blue	(900)

Story books can be left uncoded. It is recommended that colours be used singly and not in combination. The basic limitation to the use of colour lies in the affirmation that one male in eight suffers from colour blindness in one form or another. The most difficult colours are blue and green; this might suggest the use of, say, a green star for science in contrast to circular stick-on labels for the others. This still keeps all science books, whether they deal with weather, water, stars, flowers, trees, birds or animals, with a single symbol; the confusion which could arise would be in the use of several shapes to distinguish between books on weather, water, stars, etc.

The five subject groupings give a general introduction to the main classes of Dewey but the change in the junior school library from colour to a numerical notation may at first be difficult for some pupils; even so, one should be careful not to underestimate the ability of junior school pupils to work with the Dewey classification scheme.

The two schemes can be linked through the subject index by using subject index cards made from mounting card in the same colours as those used in the infant school central collection. In the subject list above, where a yellow sticker was used on books about transport, subject entries with a classification number in the 300s would be made on yellow cardboard strips. If the nature books had a green sticker then all entries in the 500s and 600s would be on green cardboard strips. Tier and shelf guides could also make use of the colours.

New libraries can be overwhelming at any stage of educational development; with a larger stock in the junior school library and the resultant need to accommodate them in a different way so that, with only spines showing, many of the books appear to have lost their individuality, this combination of procedures can give some confidence to those recently transferred from the infant department.

Before embarking on such a scheme, however, the librarian should be aware of the third type of subject index using colour coding for media rather than for subjects.

Colour coding: the strip index (commercially produced)

There is a body of opinion which holds that the use of colour coding in the catalogue to draw attention to the different media is an act of separation of media contrary to the spirit and purpose of the resource centre, which is the library in its modern form.

This seems to be a rather foreshortened view of the reason for introducing a variety of media into the library: they are there because they have to be different in order to perform their individual and specialized functions. It will not do to try to equate them verbally solely because they have one thing in common, namely, that they are all carriers of information. It is a fact that for illustration and information there may be only one medium which will provide the motivation: individualized learning demands particularized structuring.

In using the catalogue, the teacher who specifically requires a filmloop does not want, may not have time and should not have to read through entries for records, books, tapes, illustrations, artefacts or any other material which may have only subject similarity; the inclusion of the name of the medium in the callmark still means that it has to be read. When he is looking for a specific medium, the teacher or the pupil looks for a particular colour; when the search is a more general one to find what is available, the name of the medium on the card gives this without repeated references to the key.

The strip subject index, which has a neater, more compact appearance than the pegboard index, takes the form of a metal or plastic panel 12 or 22 in high by 4, 6, 8 or 12 in wide (305 or 559 mm × 102, 152, 203 or 305 mm).

The entry is made on a strip of wood veneer covered with coloured paper, which fits into the panel. When bought, the strips are attached to a backing sheet so that they can be stripped off for inserting into the panel; they should be peeled off separately (not cut). The individual strips are available in different depths as well as different widths. In double-sided panels fully used, strips $\frac{1}{6}$, $\frac{1}{4}$ and $\frac{1}{3}$ in (4, 6 and 8 mm) will give 144, 96 and 72 entries, respectively.

Panels can be hung on desk or rotary stands or on brackets for attaching to walls, and, according to the maker, different quantities of panels can be accommodated. One maker supplies desk, wall and rotary stands to take 10, 20, 30, 40 or 50 panels as well as a book which holds only five white plastic leaves (see Plate 6). Others supply desk stands and wall brackets taking 18 and 36 panels and rotary units taking 87, 160 and 320 panels (see Plate 9).

If the anticipated need is for only 72 entries, for example, it is useless to order only one panel which, filled on both sides, will accommodate 72 strips. Initially, each side should be not more than one-third full; although this may seem extravagant it does help to avoid what to the librarian appears to be the eternal

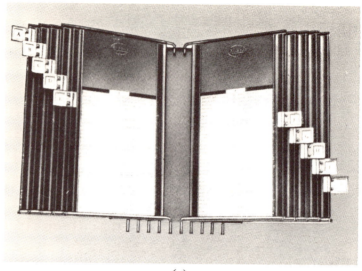

(*a*)

(*b*)

Plate 6   Strip index (a) Wall bracket (b) **Desk stand** (c) Rotary unit

(c)

moving of strips because the panels fill so quickly. This advice comes as the fruit of personal experience following an initial effort to spend carefully.

The depth of the strip used will depend to some extent on the age of the reader for whom it is provided. Since consideration of eye-span is important in the case of young children and slow readers, the worst combination of strips available for a subject index would probably be a strip 8 in (203 mm) wide by $\frac{1}{6}$ in (4 mm) deep; where vision is travelling from left to right over this span the subject word can easily be misread with the subject number for the word above or below; this is awkward enough in itself, but as far as the pupil is concerned the resultant failure in the use of the library is even more important. The user has failed, and so has the librarian.

There are two ways of using colour in the strip subject index.

1. *Plain strips with coloured stick-on labels*

It is likely that the number of media available in the library will exceed the number of colours available for use; this means an initial grouping of media. It is obvious from the pro-forma (Fig. 8, p. 81) that, in addition to books, three simple groupings are possible:

(a) illustrations including art reproductions, photographs, post-cards and charts;
(b) films, filmloops, filmstrips, slides and transparencies;
(c) records and tapes.

Where there are videotapes they can be included in (c), but provision still has to be made for games, models and specimens.

Colour Plate 2 shows how the coloured stickers are used. Because of the cost of colour reproduction, the number of colours has been restricted here to five, used as follows:

Buff	used for the strips themselves
Black	books
Red	illustrations, postcards, charts, etc.
White	films, filmloops, filmstrips, slides, etc.
Green	records and tapes

Stickers can be bought in several colours from good stationers or photographic dealers; by using either blue or green, but not both, the problem with colour blindness is lessened. As round stickers can be bought in different diameters it is advisable to check the size with the depth of the strip to ensure that the stickers do not overlap. Rectangular stickers can be cut to size but it is remarkably difficult to keep them parallel to one another.

For some time it is possible that there will be more books in the library on a subject than there are items in other media; in some cases there will only be a book. It gives substance to the classification number if the stickers for books are in the column nearest to the classification number. At the same time, however, the index shows the specificity of media other than books at children's level.

In the example illustrated the stickers are more widely spaced than they would be with more media in use. One has to be careful with the space taken by long subject entries but at the last entry, 'VOLCANOES', within the space occupied by the four stickers there is room for three more; alternatively, they could have a different spacing. In this example the strips measure $6 \times \frac{1}{3}$ in (152 × 8 mm).

If two or more types of the medium shown are in use it is better to indicate this on the sticker than to have a confusing selection of colours bespattering the panels like uncontrollable confetti. In 'celluloid' there might be films, filmloops, filmstrips, slides and transparencies; the abbreviation for each (see Fig. 8) can be inserted within the circle, neatly and always in the same order. If it happens that not enough care was taken initially when inserting the abbreviations 'F' and 'S' to allow for an unexpected addition of a filmstrip, the sticker should be peeled off and a fresh one substituted. Black was chosen for books because, in the scarcity of coloured stickers compared with the number of media, books do not need an added symbol.

Transparent protective sheets are available to protect the strips from heavy handling and dust; these are easily inserted between the strips and the side overlaps.

It is helpful to have a key to the colour coding either at the top of each 'page' or at the top left of each opposite pair.

2. *Strips of several colours*

In this type of index, each group of media has a different coloured strip: distinctions within each group are indicated by using the abbreviation for the medium followed by a stroke immediately in front of the classification number or notation (see

Colour Plate 3).

Whereas, when using the coloured stickers system, each *subject* is represented by one strip, we now have, under each subject, a coloured strip for each *group of media* represented: for instance, all films, filmloops, filmstrips, slides and overhead transparencies have a subject index entry on a white strip. It is unnecessary to allot a colour to each individual medium, such as those just listed; the overloaded effect that this would produce would be likely to overwhelm the pupil so that the index would be ignored.

Except in the case of books, the medium is indicated by its abbreviation (see Fig. 8) followed by a stroke to separate it from the notation; where two or more media within a group are represented at a particular subject the abbreviations are separated by a colon:

        SQUIRRELS   FL:S/599.3

When two media are combined in a library where the policy is to segregate the media, the combination can be kept together in a multi-media filing box (see Plate 4) and shelved with either medium. The last entry on Colour Plate 3 shows a tape accompanied by a filmstrip and shelved with the tapes, indexed thus:

        VOLCANOES : with filmstrip   T/551.2

This entry could be the result of a BBC radiovision broadcast.

The penultimate entry is for another tape on its own about volcanoes; there could be a number of reasons for the presence of this, one of which might be that it is the teacher's notes for an individual or group assignment on this subject.

A comparison of the two strip index systems

Although the number of media recorded within each subject varies, the average is just over two per subject. By halving the depth of the strip used with the coloured stickers, i.e. from $\frac{1}{3}$ to $\frac{1}{6}$ in (from 8 to 4 mm), the two examples illustrated occupy the same amount of space, namely, one side of a panel. Both examples use strips 6 in (152 mm) wide. The effect is to crowd the entries, although this is offset to some extent by the use of several colours, allowing the vision to travel left to right along the colour. It can be appreciated that the use of a single colour as the basis with the narrower strip would be more difficult and more likely to cause confusion in the reading of the notation.

If the multi-colour base is preferred the deeper strip, $\frac{1}{3}$ in (8 mm), is likely to be more effective for primary and middle school pupils. The fact that twice the amount of space will be used allows the index to spread and be seen more easily.

In both indexes block capitals have been used; many schools will prefer to use the writing taught in school or to use the lower case letters of the typewriter. This, of course, is a matter for each school to decide for itself.

Conclusion

The subject index is the key to the library; it is therefore necessary to give its construction careful consideration. The aim of the librarian is to provide a library which the pupils themselves can use.

One of the functions of the infant school is to teach the pupil to read, and he needs practice to become fluent. The visual index will contribute to this because it is there, open, all day and every day, and, to follow his interest and work on his assignments, he has to be able to read it. The pupil should be taught to find things for himself. He can learn the techniques and disciplines of library usage if his teacher will instruct him to this end; it has always been slightly ridiculous to tell the pupil he will find what he wants on the top – or is it the second top? – shelf of the bookcase beside the window looking out at the headmaster's parked car. 'It's a large red book.' Let's be honest – it seldom is.

CHAPTER TEN

Preparation and Storage of Materials

Librarians are accustomed to being teased about standing in their libraries with a stern expression, daring anyone to lay a finger on a book for fear of making the place look untidy. Yet the teaser, searching seriously for information, would have no faith in his ability to locate it in an untidy library which gives the impression that the librarian does not know what to do with what he has. So perhaps one can understand the librarian who, having had to deal only with the serried ranks of books toeing the edges of shelves and awaiting inspection, is diffident about the invasion of the unknown enemy whose only real fault lies in the apparently insoluble problem of storage.

A great deal of thought has already gone into the question of storage in a multi-media library, for it is even more important in that situation to present an appearance of straightforward simplicity. Apart from the slightly unwieldy group of spheres and models, the remainder can be dealt with by using existing bookshelves, purchasing purpose-built equipment or having some constructed.

If the librarian thinks of the number of slides in school and the fact that one bookcase shelf 30 in (762 mm) wide by 7 in (178 mm) deep will take twelve plastic slide trays each holding 35 slides, thus giving a total of 420 slides, he should begin to see the problem in perspective. As will be seen, media can be stored in close proximity in one unit while retaining their individuality; it may be more useful to deal with them now in alphabetical order.

Artefacts and specimens

Man and nature bring these two together. An artefact is an article made by man and a specimen is an article produced by nature and typical of its kind. Between them they more or less account for the term 'realia' – an imigrant term from America.

Visits to museums and similar institutions have increased considerably in recent years: the enthusiasm and help of their members of staff have had much to do with children's growing interest in artefacts and specimens – not that boys' interest was ever totally absent if the contents of their trouser pockets were any indication.

If museum visits give opportunities to see and touch, school journeys, school visits and field work give opportunities to acquire. Stamps, coins, medals, buttons, birds' eggs, wild flowers – all with many interesting aspects – can build into interesting collections, and can be made more interesting when they become the focal point of activity such as creative writing and drama. Imagination needs facts on which to build, and returns to facts for the purpose of expression. Song, mime, dance, play, painting, poetry, story, model, recording, filmstrip — all could derive from looking at a button.

Storage of artefacts and specimens

These materials are all three-dimensional – it would be risky to pronounce that a stamp is not – but some are more so than others. It might be considered safer to fix stamps into albums from the beginning; on the other hand, like coins and medals which are flat, they can be put into DWViewpacks[1] and stored as shown in Plate 15 (p. 147).

[1] Diana Wyllie Viewpacks.

Shells, buttons, geological specimens and similar objects can be kept in shallow trays or drawers. To prevent dust gathering on them they can first be inserted into polythene bags and labelled – specimen and bag. How far cataloguing is individualized is a matter for each librarian, but on the whole items tend to group themselves so as to be manageable as a collection.

Charts

Physically, charts are so uncontrollable and awkward that one tends to want to forget about them. A few are small enough to be dealt with like illustrations; for the others protection is necessary, since the slightest careless handling can quickly damage them beyond repair. Although some charts are available free of charge others are not, so protection of some kind is advisable.

Some charts can be purchased already laminated; others can be laminated commercially.[1] 'Takibak' or 'Vistafoil GB' can be used by the librarian or his helpers; the use of either of these may make a join inevitable but the appearance and life of the chart are improved.

For many years architects have used edge-binders to protect their plans. A tape is fitted into the left-hand side of the edge-binder shown in Plate 7. The chart is fed into place and when the handle is turned the tape overlaps the edge as the chart moves forward. Incorporated into the binder is a device for cutting the tape as required. The tapes are $\frac{1}{8}$ in (3 mm) wide and are available transparent or in blue, green, grey or red.

Each chart will require a hole punched at each corner and, if the chart is large, two extra holes on the top and bottom; a gummed reinforcement over each hole back and front will give additional strength.

Storage of charts

1. *With illustrations.* So long as the chart does not have to be

[1] Dunn and Wilson offer this service.

folded it can be treated, catalogued and filed as an illustration. Up to 30 × 20 in (762 × 508 mm) the chart can be filed in a plan-stand (see p. 132).

Plate 7 Edge-binder with tapes and large stapler

2. *Treated separately and dealt with as charts.* They can be stored in tubes available in different lengths from drawing office suppliers. Plastic tubes are available, but as they are almost frictionless the chart tends to slip out of the tube unless one end is blocked permanently and the other temporarily. They are more expensive than the cardboard variety with one end solid and a metal screw cap on the other. Whether the storage for the tubes is horizontal or vertical it is helpful if (a) only two lengths of tube are used and (b) there is not too much difference in their lengths.

With a diameter of 2 in (50 mm), two suitable lengths of tube are 30 in (762 mm) and 40 in (1016 mm).

Horizontal shelving. From front to back this must be deep enough to take the smaller tube; the exact length of it will bring the metal cap of the shorter tube neatly to the edge of the shelf where the identifying label can be read easily. Where larger tubes are also in use they can be shelved together either on the top shelf or, perhaps more safely, on the lowest. It is for the librarian to be on the look-out for situations which may be hazardous.

The width of the shelf must be less than the depth from front to back, so that the tubes have no opportunity to roll to the back where, at a distance of 30 in from the front, they would be a nuisance to recover. A width of 22 in (559 mm) will accommodate ten tubes and allow enough space for movement, as with books on a shelf.

It is important if charts are classified that they should not be stored in rigid sections; free on a shelf they will roll easily from side to side to allow the insertion of a new tube or the replacement of one which has been returned from loan. In rolling, the labels may not always be upright but if that offends, no one will be better pleased than the librarian if the offended one puts them straight. Flexibility is valuable and saves having to extract several tubes individually to put one in its place, as with a rigid arrangement. The only alternative would be to have an accession-number type of arrangement, and that is one order sequence which this author is unlikely to recommend. A wine-rack type of shelving has this rigidity and generally takes more space – always a valuable commodity – to accommodate the same number of tubes as the flat shallow shelf.

As the cardboard tube with a chart inside weighs only about 1 oz, the shelf to take ten tubes need not be heavy. The space between the top surface of a shelf and the underside of the one above will be the diameter of the tube plus one inch (25 mm) to give handling room. Allowing for the thickness of the shelves, a space 15 in high by 22 in wide by 30 in deep (381 × 559 × 762 mm) should give four shelves to take forty tubes 2 in (51 mm) in diameter.

So that the labels on the tubes on the lowest shelf can be read easily the bottom shelf should be not less than 15 in (381 mm) from floor level.

It may be possible to store charts, for example, in the space under one of the table tops. Figure 20 shows storage for thirty charts and is divided into squares to give an indication of storage possibilities for tubes with a diameter of 2 in (51 mm), but in practice only the horizontal division into shelves is required.

With modern plastic shelving available in DIY shops it should not be difficult to fit up something so that the identifying ends of tubes show on the side of the table away from the chair; a table 54 × 30 in (1372 × 762 mm) could be used in this way to store tubes without occupying additional floor space.

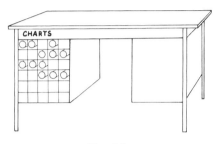

Fig. 20

It is understood that a triangular tube is on the market with two advantages over the round one: although a thin rubber band put loosely round each end of the chart before inserting it into the tube will help to extract it, because its circumference will be made smaller than the internal circumference of the tube, the triangular tube provides at the angles three places for the fingers to catch hold of the chart; and being triangular in shape, the tube will more easily remain in a stable position for reading the identifying label. It has been claimed that by using a triangular tube more can be accommodated in a given space; at some inconvenience to the users this is so, in the proportion of approximately nine to five. While the tube rests on the shelf the identifying label can always be upright but the claim in fact rests on the assumption that almost forty per cent will not rest on the shelf but be wedged apex down between those which do. With this insecure situation it will be difficult to maintain classified order.

Vertical storage. A box standing 24 in (610 mm) high will hold upright charts 30 in (762 mm) long. Such a box with an end section of about 9 × 5 in (229 × 127 mm) will take eight tubes. The local grocer may be able to provide such a box or carton;

with a little imagination and the use of some plastic covering such as Fablon, a covering can be made to camouflage the printed cardboard box, and perhaps it can even be made to resemble the bookcases. With an initial or anticipated stock of more than eight tubes, two or more boxes can be joined together. A vertical arrangement such as this can be put at the end of a bookcase as illustrated in Fig. 21. Where wall shelving is interrupted by a window the wallspace under it can be used so long as there is not a hot radiator nearby.

Fig. 21

Photographing charts for preliminary evaluation

Earlier, mention was made of the damage which can so easily be done to a chart in handling it, yet browsing is essential in order to evaluate the content and presentation. Photographed, the chart can be viewed in another form.

1. *Colour slides*. The slides of all photographed charts can be filed in classified order in individual pockets of DW viewpacks (see Plate 15). When the classification number has been found in the subject index the user will have recourse, initially, to the slides. The slide does not have to be extracted from its pocket: the Viewpack can either be held up to the light or else over a light-box to obtain a general impression. To see the details, and particularly the small print, it will be necessary to use a projector: this should not present a problem in the library where the projector and a nearby screen, or part of a wall painted white, are basic equipment.

2. *Colour prints*. These can vary considerably from the original and are dearer than slides to produce. They will last longer mounted on card and kept filed in classified order in a box near the charts.

3. *Black and white enlargement prints*. This method has been used successfully and found to be helpful in evaluating charts within a given subject area to decide which charts had no relevance, and therefore did not have to be handled, which were doubtful and required closer scrutiny using the chart itself, and lastly those which obviously contained essential material in a suitable layout. In the last instance an examination of the chart might be required. Not only is unnecessary handling considerably reduced but their accessibility in this form tends to increase the use of the charts.

The photographs themselves provide a useful reference material. Enlarged to approximately 8×10 in $(203 \times 254 \, \text{mm})$, the prints are mounted on cards 10×12 in $(254 \times 305 \, \text{mm})$; the card should be thick to reduce the possibility of their being torn, and black so that marks will not easily be seen. Use a pamphlet box $14\frac{1}{2} \times 10\frac{3}{4} \times 2\frac{1}{2}$ in $(368 \times 273 \times 63 \, \text{mm})$, as in Plate 8, and insert them in classified order with the classification number at the top left-hand corner of the mount. The turned-down front of the box allows easy access without having to extract any other than the two or three to be compared.

An ordinary camera can be used, but the better the lens the better the result should be. This is probably one of the areas where parental help will be willingly given. If a dark-room is available the opportunity to see a photographer at work may be useful, especially to the librarian. If pupils are not already using cameras in their assignments this could be a valuable introduction.

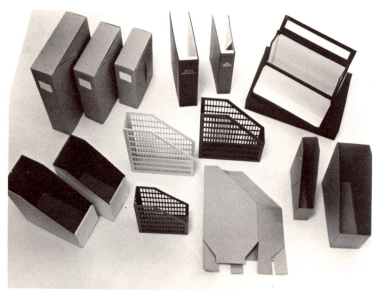

Plate 8 'Fold-flat' storage cartons (top left)
'Easi-binders' (top centre)
Greylock magazine boxes (bottom left)
Board and plastic pamphlet boxes (right and centre)

Filmstrips

A filmstrip, in black and white, coloured or tinted, is a length of film normally 35 mm wide containing a number of still camera shots. In the sequence in which they appear they may form a story or a series of steps in the development of a theme. Produced commercially in ever increasing numbers and with photographs of a high standard, they play an important part as a teaching or learning aid. They may be photographs of places, people or objects; they may be diagrams. Some are in cassettes requiring a compatible projector for viewing; others will require a filmstrip hand-viewer, a filmstrip projector or a projector which takes slides or filmstrips. Though the need for care should be demonstrated, the machines are easy for children to use and the user can progress at a pace to suit himself. Notes are usually provided.

If the teacher accepts the value of the filmstrip in the sequence of frames as they appear, he will use the notes to plan his lesson. It is more than likely, however, that while accepting all or most of the frames individually, he will not accept their sequence; no two teachers approach the teaching of a subject in exactly the same way. While the teacher is presented with a problem, it is the solution which affects the viewer.

A common method of dealing with this is to roll the frames to and fro in the projector to give a sequence acceptable to the teacher concerned. The more able pupils may remain with him through this marathon but the less able will soon be lost, leaving many children at different levels of comprehension and the teacher having expended time and energy. Unfortunately, as a result, too many teachers by-pass the filmstrip; although one can appreciate the frustration, it seems an unnecessarily drastic step to take with potentially valuable material.

Filmstrips into slides

If the filmstrip is cut into separate frames and put into slide mounts, which can be bought from a good photographic dealer, the opportunity is provided to re-arrange the slides in any order, or to select only those suitable; this is particularly convenient for individual assignments. (For further details, see the section on slides.) The possibilities for use of the frames have now greatly increased, gaining strength from, and giving support to, material already in the slide collection.

Whether the filmstrip remains as an entity or not, there is still the detail of cataloguing. For example, it may not be known to a teacher dealing with the division of common fields into furlongs that the twelfth, thirteenth and fourteenth frames of part one of a series of five filmstrips on the English parish church show a map of Toddington drawn by Thomas Agas in 1581. It may be that these are the only frames worth recording in the catalogue in a particular school. It so happens that, in this instance, there is an index to the frames as well as pamphlets with copious notes; this leaves an open-ended situation with all sorts of possibilities. As a filmstrip, the cataloguing is simple; as individual slides, the work will certainly increase. The decision should be made on the best use of the material; if it means more work then the librarian may need more voluntary help.

New problems created

The breaking-up of filmstrips into individual slides introduces some problems of organization for the librarian. When the slides from the filmstrip are ready to be classified and catalogued they may be kept in a slide box, or in a carousel labelled as a unit, in which case provision must be made to draw attention to slides catalogued individually, as described above. If slides can be borrowed from the general collection, what will happen to a set like this if parts of it are borrowed? This question may help to decide whether the library should become a reference workroom.

If an individual slide is treated as a separate unit, and so classified to gain from its proximity to similar related material, an indication of its association with, and placing in, the original filmstrip can be given on the mount. Alternatively, the individual callmark showing slideset, classification and accession number may be shown against the numerical sequence in the filmstrip notes, so that the slides can be easily reassembled if required.

There are no 'correct' answers to such problems: no librarian can please everyone, but it is his job to make the decisions and to know and believe in his reasons.

Filmstrip notes

Whether the notes accompanying filmstrips are detailed or merely outlines, the use made of them needs scrutiny and particularly for individual learning situations. At best it is of little value to present the less able pupil, and particularly the slow reader, with a filmstrip to watch and a booklet of notes to read. He cannot look at both at once and he may not have the staying power to deal with the notes, so he will try to get by on his own interpretation of the images he sees.

On the other hand, if a collection of slides, or a filmstrip, is accompanied by a commentary recorded in simple language in a voice he can recognize, the pupil's attention may be concentrated and he will probably become more personally involved in his assignment: instead of having his sense of sight diverted in two directions, he makes use of sight and hearing simultaneously.

Storage of filmstrips

In a unified library there can be no justification for accessible books and inaccessible filmstrips; the latter can be openly shelved. As power points are still usually on the walls it will be convenient to have projectors near them and possible to have light shelving on the walls to take the filmstrips. According to the number of filmstrips already in the school, and doubling that number for future expansion, a simple shelf unit can be made. Each shelf 12 in (305 mm) long will take six filmstrips; 24 in (610 mm) long, it will take thirteen (see Figs 22 and 23). The depth of the shelf from front to back is the same as the height of the upright container, approximately $1\frac{3}{4}$ in (44 mm).

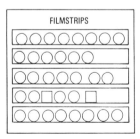

Fig. 22

A hook at each end of the top of the case will hold the top close to the wall, and a strut about $1\frac{1}{2}$ in (38 mm) fixed to the lowest part of the back will push it out from the wall to tilt the whole unit, so that containers do not fall forward. Placed on their sides, the containers will roll easily to allow the insertion of those returned from use into their classified placings; the tops with the identifying information will face outward, while the bottoms of the containers will be against the back of the unit.

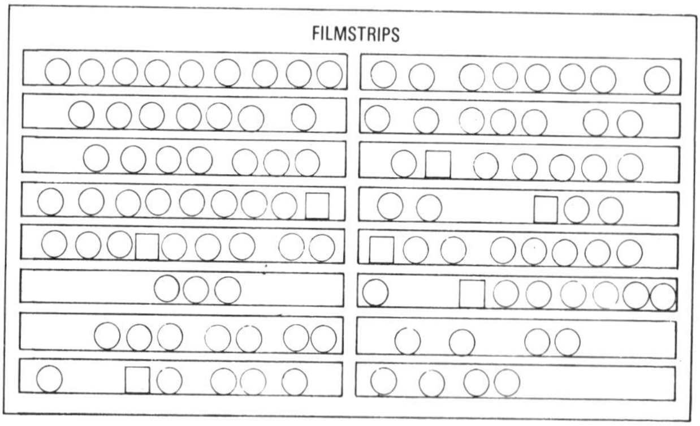

Fig. 23

Another method is to slope the shelf higher at the front than the back so that the back of the shelf unit is flat against the wall and no strut is needed at the bottom; the containers will naturally be tilted backwards (see Fig. 24). In this case, therefore, the depth of the shelf will be a fraction greater. There need not be more than $2\frac{3}{4}$ in (70 mm) beween the top of one shelf and the underside of the one above.

Hardboard is strong enough for the shelving but if a more substantial fitting is wanted care should be taken not to make it appear too heavy; ten filmstrips in containers weigh very little. The appearance of the unit, particularly if it is made of hardboard, will be improved by painting or staining it.

When fixed to the wall the top shelf should be within reach of everyone who is likely to use it. A more useful purpose may be

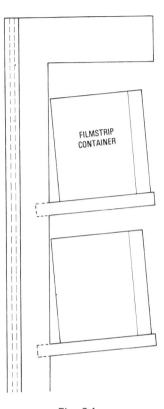

FILMSTRIP
CONTAINER

Fig. 24

served by having a wide unit with two shelves rather than one half as wide and twice as high.

A similar system is illustrated in Plate 9 which shows a plastic tray[1] with five divisons to take about thirty filmstrips. It can remain flat, be fixed to a wall framework or be used at an angle within an existing bookcase as in Figs 28 and 30. Inside each division of this tray a piece of foam rubber holds the filmstrip containers firmly, but still allowing for easy extraction.

Filmstrip containers can be kept in shallow drawers made for

[1] Available from Don Gresswell Ltd.

this purpose and produced in sets of four, eight, twelve or sixteen-drawer cabinets. Obviously, access is more restricted with this method and the more drawers in the cabinet the more restricted the access. If this method is preferred it would therefore be worth considering the purchase of two four-drawer cabinets rather than one of eight, in spite of the extra cost. These cabinets are made by several manufacturers of office equipment; Plate 10 shows one made by Stor, who offer an alternative to their stone-grey enamel finish with a choice of six colours. The drawers are on suspension slides and the cabinets are available with or without locks.

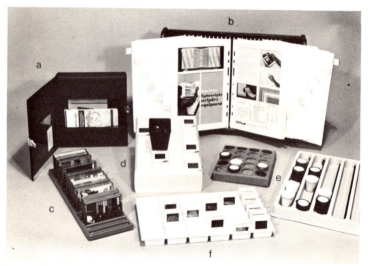

Plate 9 (a) Multi-media box
       (b) Desk stand with plastic panels for catalogue
       (c) Catalogue drawer insert for cassettes
       (d) Light-box with magnifier
       (e) Filmstrip trays
       (f) Drawer insert for slides

To keep some kind of order, removable divisions with equally-spaced slots are available to give storage space for thirty-six containers. Although plastic inserts for slides are available it is still possible to have a mixture of slides and filmstrips because the divisions are small.

A cardboard nest for filmstrip containers is shown in Plate 9; although the containers themselves should hold it upright, it can be strengthened at the corners to keep it from splaying in a drawer. Again, for those who like filmstrips in drawers, this is a useful, inexpensive solution.

Plate 10   Stor metal cabinet for filmstrips and slides

Where filmstrips are likely to be viewed over a light-box or held up to daylight a PVC Viewpack for 35 mm strips is available from Diana Wyllie Ltd. It has six horizontal compartments, each approximately $11\frac{1}{2}$ in (292 mm) wide. Once inside the compartment, the strip is protected from fingering and dust.

Storage of filmstrip notes

In a library pamphlets receive harsh treatment unless they are protected, and filmstrip notes are no exception. It is not usually difficult to buy a replacement copy of the notes but a little care when they first arrive will prevent early disintegration. This is simply done by making a cover of pliable card and stapling it to the notes, using a long-arm stapler and making sure that the ends of the staple are in the centre fold of the notes rather than on the outside of the cover, where they might cause scratches to hands.

On a piece of white paper pasted to the outside of the cover put the callmark showing medium (i.e. filmstrip), classification number and accession number as they appear on the lid of the filmstrip container; under this put the heading used for the filmstrip.

There is no clear answer to the many-sided problem of the storage of filmstrip notes. The librarian of the modern primary and middle school library is concerned with the retrieval of information at any time of the day so he will have to find a solution to fit his own circumstances.

1. The notes can be filed in a pamphlet box such as any of those illustrated in Plate 8. They are easily found if kept in classified order and when more than one container is used the contents should be clearly and neatly noted on the outside of each.

2. They can be kept in one of the drawers of the type of cabinet mentioned above, but it must be remembered that for every drawer full of filmstrips two will probably be required for the notes.

3. They can be filed in classified order in a ring binder.

4. If taped they can be filed with cassettes. (See p. 152).

5. Among the items illustrated in Plate 4 is a box to take the filmstrip and the notes. It can be placed upright on a shelf and keeps the two components together; if these may be borrowed, the issue card can be kept inside the box while they are not on loan.

Wherever the filmstrips are accommodated there should be a statement on or beside the unit giving the siting of the notes.

Illustrations

For many years wallcharts have been part of the equipment of most classrooms and they have long been established as a valuable visual aid; usually well produced, they save members of staff the time-consuming and repetitive task of drawing or tabulating on the blackboard material which is better produced commercially, and more effective. Similar illustrative material of various kinds has been acquired by schools and classrooms and it is unfortunate that so much of this potentially valuable material has inevitably suffered from unsuitable handling, mainly for want of appropriate storage facilities.

In the library this medium will probably expand more quickly than any other; it will probably also be the one on which the greatest demands will be made, partly because it can be used as it is, needing no machine to make it effective. This type of material will last longer if given some kind of protective treatment before making it available for general use. Although the kinds of illustration available in each school may differ it is proposed to offer some suggestions for storage in the hope that this may solve one of the problems facing the librarian.

Offering a service

There may have to be a good deal of groundwork done before embarking on the project and before colleagues hand over their collections; it may help the librarian to 'sell' his idea if he finds an illustration which he intends to add to the collection and mounts it on heavy paper or card, as described later, to serve as an example of the proposed standard. From the outset he should let it be understood that only those items which are in good condition and up-to-date will be acceptable or that he will be free to make his own decisions on receiving them. It will be as well for him to realize, also, that the best from each classroom may not be forthcoming for some time, perhaps until his standard has been assessed.

Collecting material

The librarian should work out with his colleagues some kind of procedure for collecting material. Their co-operation is natural, useful and essential but unless there is a plan it is likely either that the contributions will come in multiple copies, because several members of staff read the same periodicals, or that very little will be forthcoming.

Individual classes can be asked to take responsibility for certain areas of interest such as art and architecture, local history, local development, foreign countries, science and nature study, transport, etc. These will overlap to some extent, but duplicates of some material may be useful; the time taken to prepare this material will probably be the deciding factor.

Collecting illustrations usually generates much interest, particularly among the children who play a leading role in their use. In finding the illustrations children may sometimes read the articles concerned, and an individual pupil may be able to make, in his own words, a cassette tape of the narrative linking a group of pictures. This kind of background information is also helpful in classification, though the librarian may in fact prefer to have the whole original article or periodical. Before rushing into a decision, however, he would be well advised to wait until he has assessed the amount of work involved in the library as a whole: there are few sights more discouraging than bundles of periodicals waiting to be gone through for illustrative material, and there is the accompanying problem of the seemingly endless requests from colleagues who want to use material they have passed to the librarian.

Size of mounts

Consideration will have to be given to the sizes of mounts to be used and to how they will be accommodated. The contents of the collection are easier to handle if two or three standard sizes are used; two could be agreed, even if it means putting more than one picture on some mounts. For example, there might be an article on lions with several different photographs showing, on one, the lion itself, on another the cubs and on a third the whole family. Two, or perhaps all three, might be put on one mount. A grouping such as this might well have more impact than each alone. Of course, understanding and judgment are necessary to avoid a jumble of subjects on one card, assembled simply because the shapes of the illustrations fitted.

The subject resulting from any grouping will have to be

decided for classification purposes so that illustrations can be retrieved easily from the filing system when they are required.

Storage of illustrations

From habit, when one thinks of storage for material of this kind, one tends to think in terms of plan chests with a series of wide, shallow drawers which will ensure that items, because they are held down by the weight of others on top of them, will remain flat and so be easily handled. Yet anyone who has used this kind of equipment knows how difficult it is to move the contents to find what is sought and how easy it is for the smaller items to be lost. He no doubt also knows how easy it is, even when taking care, to receive a deep cut on one's finger because the paper edge is so sharp.

Lateral filing may be preferable so that, in assembling and classifying material under subjects, a folder can be used to accommodate a certain coverage of subjects in the way that a shelf in a bookcase accommodates a particular subject coverage of books. Just as a shelf guide at the left-hand end of a shelf shows the subject content of the books there, so there will be a guide to the subject content on the outside of the folder. If the size of the folder, or envelope, approximates to the maximum size of the mounts on which illustrations are pasted it is probable that two sizes of folder will suffice; the great majority of the mounts can also be of these two sizes. Small mounts can be difficult to find among larger ones and they are also remarkably easy to lose.

Railex produce a strong folder with a metal fitting at the top, like a coat hanger, which hangs from a rail; the folder has a slanted fold so that when it is unhooked from the shelf and lying flat on a table the extrication of the mounts is simple. A folder taking card mounts up to 18×15 in (457×381 mm) and expanding to a thickness of one inch (25 mm) will hold 25–30 mounts: a three foot run (914 mm) of rail which will take up to thirty folders will therefore accommodate 800–900 mounted illustrations. Some files expand beyond one inch, but when they are filled their weight makes them difficult to handle. Steel cabinets are available in a variety of heights, with or without

Plate 11   Railex plan-stand

doors or roller blinds, to take the different sizes of folders.

The Railex plan-stand illustrated in Plate 11 is designed with a double rail (see Fig. 25) to take large folders which hang with two hooks because of the weight of the folder when it is full. This size, with the advantage of being able to take large and small illustrations, is useful as a preliminary purchase. It takes about fifteen folders and may be all that some schools will need initially. When the collection outgrows the first plan-stand, that will be the time to extract all mounts smaller than 18 × 15 in (457 × 381 mm) to try to estimate the speed and the way in which it will grow — whether expansion will continue on the plan-stand dimensions or whether a steel cabinet should be bought for the smaller mounts. A cabinet 40 in (1016 mm) high will take approximately 1700 mounted illustrations on two levels of rails.

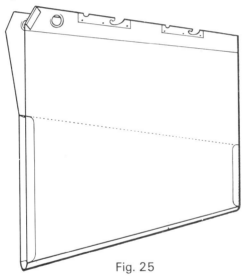

Fig. 25

In price there is not much to choose between the two systems. At the outset, the plan-stand is cheaper but the folders dearer; it must be remembered, however, that in capacity the filing cabinet will eventually take almost four times the number of folders taken by the plan-stand. One cannot really make a straight comparison. The librarian should guard against finding himself with a half-empty cabinet which can so easily and so quickly become the receptacle for all sorts of junk.

In the case of the tall cabinets it is usually cheaper to buy an initial unit and, later, an extension to attach to it than to buy two separate initial units.

Guidance for helpers

It is of little use starting to think of standards halfway through the exercise; these must be set at the beginning. The librarian is responsible for standards, so he must set them and ensure that the whims of individual helpers do not cause unforeseen difficulties. He would be wise to discuss suggestions, but in the end he will use his own judgment.

Care must be taken when extracting material from periodicals; first remove the staples and then trim material either with a ruler and scissors or with a guillotine. Extraneous matter should be excluded. The librarian will decide at what stage in the processing the necessary cataloguing details should be recorded on the back of the mount. It is important that the general subject matter of the illustration is recorded here, even if the information on the front of the mount refers to a specific detail of the picture. It is probably unnecessary to show the name of the periodical and, except in certain circumstances, the date, on the front of the mount.

When mounted, the illustration should have the same space on the left as on the right, and the space at the lower edge should be greater than the space at the top to allow for the caption and the addition of such explanatory matter as is considered suitable. It is helpful to try placing the illustration on the mount before applying the paste; when it seems to be placed satisfactorily, put a light pencil mark on the mount at each corner of the illustration. This way it need not be a messy job to place it finally.

Those who do this part of the work (see p. 40) may have their own preferences for adhesives but Gloy, thinly applied, gives good results; a clean duster should be used to press the illustration firmly in position. Pasting can be done on top of old newspapers; a considerable supply of these is useful for it is false economy to place a fresh illustration on top of a sheet of paste-sodden newspaper so that it is unsightly before it is mounted. Lots of old newspapers, clean dusters always washed after use, and many washings of hands are necessary to be certain of a clean finish to the work.

Either before or after the mounting process, punch a hole in each corner of the mount about one inch (25 mm) in from the two near edges. This acts as a veiled suggestion for the insertion of drawing pins, and thus a protection against unnecessary damage to the mount. There will be times when at least one of the holes will be beyond the pin-up area where it is to be displayed, just as there will be individualists who want to do things their own way, but the presence of the holes should help. When the mounting card is being ordered it may be possible to have the holes punched by machine before delivery.

As with the bookstock, it is useful to have the name of the school stamped either on the front or back. It can be done neatly and unobtrusively on the lower front area or else on the back and out of the way.

Allowances have to be made for the appearance of unintentional dirty marks, some of which can be rubbed off while others are too greasy to treat successfully. When it is obvious from the beginning that the illustration will be of long term value it may be worth considering the use of some kind of transparent adhesive covering such as Takibak or Vistafoil GB, already mentioned in connection with bookjackets. There is an art in handling this material but it is worth the effort. When covering illustrative material there should be an overlap to the back of at least half an inch (13 mm).

Except perhaps in the case of art reproductions the initial cost of this medium is low on average; it would be a pity, therefore, not to consider this type of protection for the most valuable items.

Models

No picture can substitute for the experience of handling a three-dimensional object. A television programme about the launching of a spacecraft is there and gone, all within a short period of time; later, after the landing, children – and adults – peer so closely at the television screen that one fears for the safety of the astronauts lest they and the capsule be picked off the screen and put on the floor for a closer look. The launching of a spacecraft is one of those happenings where we are limited to a two-dimensional view. A model provides the opportunity for personal involvement.

The pupil may never be likely to board a cabin cruiser but the library can give him the opportunity of trying his skill on the model of the canal lock. The crusader, the puritan and the Jacobite become more convincing as models. The take-apart model of the heart must mean more than the ghostly, insubstantial reproduction on an overhead projector transparency. Farm and railway models, ships, aircraft, cars for pleasure and road safety instruction – the possibilities are extensive.

Relief models are likely to be present in the library. Normally they are lightweight and can be easily moved. When they are not part of the library display they should be kept in polythene bags to protect them from the dust; alternatively, a perspex cover can be made which allows a clear view of the model and looks tidier (see Plate 2).

In themselves models are conspicuous enough so there seems to be no advantage in spending time on their classification. They can be recorded in the subject index and where no classification has been given the word 'Model' in the place where the classification number would have appeared will suffice.

Storage of models

Assuming that the bookcases are not high, the librarian might consider the usefulness of linking the storage of the models with the classification scheme in so far as they could be placed on the tops of bookcases containing books on similar or related subjects. Low uprights and shelves with a top, canopy shelf are available[1] and if a double-sided unit is bought this canopy shelf

[1] From Terrapin Reska.

gives a table-top effect. Large books and models could occupy the shelves, in which case each shelf should be a minimum of 10 in (254 mm) deep.

Some models with large bases may require special shelving, and if they are light in weight slatted shelving may be strong enough. If this is to be incorporated into the library it should be painted.

A label bearing the subject word used in the subject index should be neatly and unobtrusively fixed to the model.

Periodicals

There may not be many periodicals in the library but if there are any, their storage, like that of all the other materials, needs consideration. So often they are dumped, only to be picked up and dumped elsewhere, until they become the biggest eyesore in the library. There is no need for this kind of situation to arise.

The current issue of every periodical taken should be on display in the library and anyone who wants to read it should be able to read it there. It should be displayed in its own place and preferably not on top of a table, or on top of the catalogue cabinet where other things are piled on top of it until the periodical is in tatters.

Covers are available with stout board backs, rexine leather-cloth binding, transparent fronts of medium-thickness plastic and an elasticated cord; these are in three sizes and are not expensive. A periodicals wall rack, 'Spectrum', is shown in Plate 12; this is available[1] in different sizes and single and double-sided free-standing styles.

Storage of back numbers of periodicals

Back numbers of periodicals are often kept longer than is necessary, but at least they can be kept tidily. The two Greylock open magazine boxes shown in Plate 8 (despatched flat and

[1] From Don Gresswell Ltd.

Plate 12 Spectrum periodicals wall-rack

boxed up by the purchaser) are available in three sizes:

$7\frac{1}{4} \times 2 \times 9$ in ($184 \times 51 \times 229$ mm)
$7\frac{3}{8} \times 4 \times 10\frac{1}{4}$ in ($187 \times 102 \times 260$ mm)
$9 \times 4 \times 11$ in ($229 \times 102 \times 279$ mm)

The two illustrated on the right of the plate are not so substantial.

There is really no excuse for untidiness when this kind of equipment is available.

Photographs

Photographs appear in a variety of shapes and sizes for different reasons. Normally the photograph does not need a machine for personal viewing but the use of an episcope is often helpful for group viewing.

Photographs taken during a project are often conveniently mounted in small groups. It is advisable to use adhesive rather than corner mounts which are purpose-made for personal photograph albums and which, where there is much general use, allow the photographs to be easily extracted. Unless the librarian ensures that the weight of the mount is much heavier than the weight of the photographic paper, the photographs are by no means secure within corner mounts.

Postcards

Animals, architecture, art reproductions, birds, flowers, local history, portraits, transport of all descriptions, trees, views of this and other countries: so extensive is the cover and so wide the interests of pupils, teachers and friends that this collection will compete strongly with the illustrations collection in its growth and subject coverage. Postcards are cheaper to buy than slides are to produce and they need no machine for viewing.

Singly or in related groups they can be mounted as illustrations. On the other hand they can form a collection on their own, classified and filed upright in a strong box slightly larger than the postcards themselves. They can be filed in catalogue drawers which must be able to take a card 6 × 4 in (152 × 102 mm).

Once this collection is known to exist it will grow and this is why it should be organized in the same manner as other materials. The label, neatly fixed to the top left corner, should be small but large enough to take the callmark clearly, including the accession number.

Records

It is difficult to imagine a school without records. Instrumental, orchestral, vocal, recordings of bird songs, poetry, plays and stories for children are being produced in ever-increasing numbers. The variety is considerable: no steam railway enthusiast can be unaware of the recordings which will interest him.

Recordings other than those intended to be listened to by large groups can be obtrusive and pervasive because there are not many areas in schools which are soundproof. Where records have to be used in the library it will be necessary to have a record player which can take headphones or a junction box with several sets of ear pieces. One interesting and potentially economical development is that many young people do not like having their hair disturbed by headphones so one ear piece is held against one ear while the other ear piece goes unused. Some sets can therefore be separated into two individual ear pieces. Care is essential, however, and anyone who is not absolutely certain how to do this should consult an electrician.

Where both mono and stereo records are available in the library some precautions may have to be taken.

Storage of records

Records need careful storage; they should always stand on edge and never lie flat. Most people are aware of the normal kinds of rack and case available. Ordinary deep book shelving can be used so long as there are upright fixed divisions approximately every six inches (152 mm).

A new type of storage is now available as a lockable cabinet to take 160 records, a free-standing open unit to take 250, or else the rails and fittings to construct one's own using Spur wallstrips. Plate 13 shows a unit built in this way. For each record there is a plastic sleeve with a pocket for the issue card of the type shown in Figs 2, 3 and 4. The sleeve hangs from a channel which is obtainable in a choice of six different colours. Like coat hangers on a rod in a wardrobe, the whole slides freely along the rail to make selection easy.

Plate 13   Record storage

Shops and sometimes libraries display only the sleeves of records, while the records themselves are kept out of the way; apart from any other reasons against this procedure, the librarian must remember that he may not always be in the library to retrieve the record required.

Slides

Money available in primary schools has not encouraged the building up of collections of slides; middle schools may have a better prospect because, broadly speaking, their appearance has almost coincided with the development of the school library as a multi-media resource centre.

Making slides out of one filmstrip can produce from thirty-five to one hundred slides. With such a figure, the prospect of a slide collection begins to be a reality with which the librarian has to come to grips.

A number of project packs issued recently have included slides giving a useful range of transparent photographs which, as a whole, the individual teacher would be unlikely to acquire, since examples can cover a wide area, or a distant area, of the country; this is accentuated when the coverage is extended to other countries.

Art galleries and museums sell slides of high quality and while it is not by any means implied that the slide serves the same purpose as the art print, it may be worth a visit to the nearest gallery or museum to find out what is there. Catalogues of such slides are available, as are those from commercial suppliers with a different subject coverage.

For large group viewing the slide projector is essential, but for pupils working on individual or small group assignments the viewing is more likely to be done using a light-box (with or without a magnifier) and small handviewers. If the area of the top of the light-box is 15 × 12 in (381 × 305 mm) it will take the DW Viewpack 24. Light-boxes are simple to make with the tubes attached to the sides of the box; for those who need details of construction, R. T. B. Lamb's book, *Filmstrip and slide projectors in teaching and training*,[1] might be useful.

Several light-boxes are on the market; one is shown in Plate 3 and another in Plate 9. Plate 14 shows a DW Viewpack 24 transferred from suspension filing to a purpose-made light-box. There is a wide range of handviewers for use with mains or

[1] Published by the National Committee for Audio-visual Aids in Education.

Plate 14 Suspension filing transferred from cabinet to light-box

batteries, and several daylight ones from the very cheap to the more expensive. Any good photographic dealer will be able to advise.

Mounts for slides

When it is proposed to cut up filmstrips a supply of mounts[1] will have to be bought. Before making a purchase the librarian should check the number of double frame and single frame mounts he requires. If he is planning to use the self-adhesive type he should not buy more than he will use within a short space of time. Some packaging carries a time expiry date which should be carefully checked; and the librarian should be wary of reduced-price offers in photographic dealers' shops.

[1] Available from Diana Wyllie Ltd.

Mounts can be bought either completely blank or with the trade name on one side. One of the drawbacks of commercially produced slides is the amount of space which the producer manages to occupy with print; obviously these mounts are intended for personal use rather than for large collections which have to be organized.

There are several types of mount in the 2×2 in $(51 \times 51$ mm) size:

1. Plastic or cardboard mounts without glass
2. Plastic mounts with glass
3. Glass mounts

Cardboard mounts, which are the cheapest, are self-adhesive and take writing in ink; like books, they soil if pupils are not trained to handle them carefully. In these mounts the slide tends to 'pop' shortly after insertion into the projector, so a few seconds should be allowed to elapse before focusing. The slides are not protected from dust or finger marks.

Plastic mounts are less easily damaged round the edges, but again, without glass, the slides are unprotected from dust and finger marks. To take the callmark and a statement of the subject of the slide they require a self-adhesive label like the one in Fig. 12. Those with glass are susceptible to Newton's rings if the glass is not specially made to control this.

Glass or glass-enclosed mounts are more expensive and liable to break if dropped. They too need a label for the callmark, etc.

When the librarian asks the slide enthusiast which is the best he will almost certainly be told that it is the glass mount and in certain circumstances this is undoubtedly true. The decision will certainly lie with each school, according to circumstances. At a time when such money as was available was needed to increase the stock of software the author built up a considerable collection of slides almost entirely in cardboard mounts; some were original mounts, some were cut-up filmstrips and some were remounts because the original writing could not be deciphered or had no system in the order in which it had been presented on the mount. These lasted well, over a number of years.

So that slides can be inserted easily and correctly into projectors or viewers, the mount should be marked. Make sure that the glossy side of the film is nearest, then, having turned the picture upside down, put a spot – not just a dot – on the top right-hand corner. When the projectionist stands behind the projector this spot is on the top right-hand corner as he puts the slide into the carrier; when inserting the slide into a hand viewer this spot will be in the bottom left-hand corner. Figures 26 and 27 show how

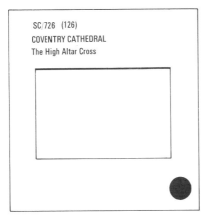

SC/726 (126)
COVENTRY CATHEDRAL
The High Altar Cross

Fig. 26

SC/598.8 (23)
WHITETHROAT
Nest and eggs

Fig. 27

the placing of the heading will be influenced by the space around the frame. Whether the spot is obvious while the slide is in the slidebox is immaterial; but the heading should be readable in this position and in the Viewpack or other slide folder such as the Brainos.

Storage of slides

The manner in which slides will be viewed will be a guide for plans for storage. To take an extreme case, suppose that all slides are in slidesets for individual viewing so that there will probably be no need to extract slides after they have been inserted into PVC folders. They could be stored in a filing cabinet (Plate 15a) or in an album (Plate 15b). The cabinet with twenty-four slides to a folder will accommodate more than 3500 slides in each drawer; the album will take 400. If slides are arranged in classified order this method entails a constant transferring of slides from one pocket to another to maintain the order when new additions have to be inserted.

In a library where the resources are in constant demand for their subject content it is useful to have the slides arranged in order of the classification in use for the other media. Slide trays with tops, or slideboxes, can be bought to keep on open shelves; they can be used for certain subject areas and clearly marked, e.g.

582.13		582.16		582.13 – 582.16
FLOWERS	or	TREES	or	FLOWERS and TREES

Start with each box about one-third full to allow for expansion and to postpone unnecessary movement. The plastic slidebox taking 35 slides can sit end-on on the normal bookshelf in the library; larger boxes may have to sit sideways. It is important, however, that if a heavy wooden box is used it should occupy a static position and not be moved by pupils. Plate 9 shows a plastic insert for a drawer.

When slides are withdrawn from their classified sequence to form a group with its own subject coverage it is helpful if this has a heading of its own to reassure the pupil he has the correct

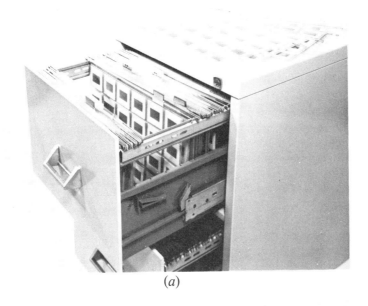

(a)

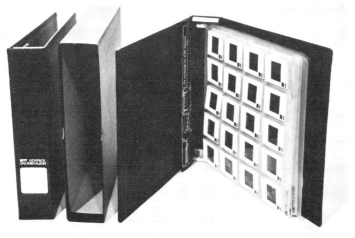

(b)

Plate 15 Storage of slides
(a) Vertical filing cabinet (b) Album

package. Kodak produce a blank slide with a matt surface[1] which can be written or drawn on with fibre-tipped or other such pens or pencils. Sometimes ballpoint pens will make blobs which are unsightly when projected, but a suitable combination of one's own style of handwriting and a particular pen will evolve with practice.

Tapes

The wide range of uses to which tape recordings are put makes their presence in schools increasingly inevitable. Before the advent of cassette tapes, which has been one of the revolutionary developments in education in recent years, the medium was surrounded by a number of difficulties. The simplicity of handling cassette and machine and the growing range of pre-recorded cassettes will make it preferable for use particularly for individual learning.

A few years ago tape recording had a battle against the record; the stereo enthusiast defends the quality of his material against all comers. But in schools which have stereo equipment which has cost a lot of money it is not by any means freely accessible to the pupils. The pupil may nearly always be denied the opportunity to hear music played on this equipment when he wants to, because he has to have a key for the room in which it is locked; he has to find an adult who is allowed to have the key and he has to find him when he has the time and the inclination to wait until the pupil has heard all that he wants to hear.

Some teachers are concerned about the quality of cassette recordings because they feel that the pupils should hear only the best recorded speech and music. But injured outcries about quality must be considered in relation to a number of mundane restrictions which are part and parcel of financial and environmental realities of many of our schools.

The cassettes available are known as C30, C60, C90 and C120, with total playing times for the two sides of each of 30, 60, 90 and 120 minutes, respectively. The difficulty of listing and,

[1] Ektagraphic Write-on Slides, available in boxes of 100.

later, reading, the contents of individual cassettes can be as difficult as it is with reel-to-reel tapes. As far as possible, therefore, it is best to use a tape with a playing time just in excess of what is required for one item. If the recording time will be twenty minutes, for instance, the tape to use is the C60 with a thirty-minute playing time on each side. There is no point in using a C90 and then adding another recording later to fill up the space.

Many teachers, primarily concerned with the communication of knowledge and the limited ability of certain individuals or groups to absorb information from printed documents, find the fact of copyright difficult to accept when the media of communication so eminently meet these needs. The initiative taken by the Council for Educational Technology resulted, at the beginning of 1974, in an arrangement whereby a local education authority, on payment of a fee, is given a blanket licence for its teachers to copy, for educational purposes, nearly all muscial records and tapes. A separate licence allows teachers' centres and resource centres to record extracts for distribution. The copying of material in books and periodicals is still bound by the Copyright Act. In any case the librarian should ask his headmaster to check the arrangements which obtain in the local education authority regarding the copying of any material.

Taping school broadcasts

Forthcoming radio and television broadcasts for schools are advertised well in advance. Every teacher knows the problem so inaccurately expressed as: 'Broadcasts for schools never fit into the time-table'. Even when a programme can be listened to when first broadcast, it may be wanted later by a teacher who did not hear it initially, or wanted as a replay when follow-up work has been done after the first hearing.

The BBC allows a tape-recording of a schools broadcast to be held for one year (radiovision for three years) and from this it may be safe to assume that a series may be held complete for that period. Unfortunately the BBC at present does not allow teachers' centres or resource centres to copy educational broadcasts for distribution to schools. This would appear to express a surprising unawareness of the time available to teachers, and the lack of technical or ancillary staff, in primary and middle schools for this kind of provision. Who will make these recordings? It seems rather ridiculous, also, for a large number of schools to tape for hypothetical use all broadcasts for the primary, middle or secondary school section. Is it possible to find a simple solution which would keep expenditure in time and money to a minimum and yet be effective?

The teachers' centre seems well situated to give this service. It is assumed that every centre will have a technician on its staff and a four-track tape recorder as part of its equipment. Provided the tape used is long enough to last through a morning or an afternoon, the machine can more or less be left through each of the sessions. The holding of tapes for a period of time will probably depend on the money available. It may be possible to hold master tapes through four terms before cleaning them to start re-using them for new broadcasts. On the other hand, it may be necessary to use them afresh at the start of each new term.

Following the publication of the forthcoming broadcast programmes schools can be asked to submit to the teachers' centre, before the beginning of the following term, a list of the recordings they want to have available in school: this does not affect the making of a master copy of the broadcast but it does help the technician to plan his work. It will not necessarily preclude a request later for a copy of a broadcast not originally asked for, but this might have to be refused, particularly if master tapes can only be held for one term.

The teachers' centre may have to insist on the deposit of a tape for each single or double broadcast and perhaps of a certain length of tape, with the making of the recording conditioned by the receipt of an appropriate tape. Alternatively, the cost of the tape may be submitted by the centre to the local education authority as a charge against the school's annual allowance.

In the case of a series, the school might want the broadcasts arranged compactly with one broadcast on each side of a tape; this could entail waiting until both sides of a tape were used.

Alternatively, the second side of each tape in a series could be used for an entirely different series, recorded on different days, which would bring both series more quickly into the school. Or the series could be recorded in any case always on one side only so that the other was left free for a teacher's comments, notes or suggestions for groups or individual work in connection with it.

Let us take this further and suggest that, for the first recording in every series, the first side of the tape be left free to be used for the teacher's introduction to the series, to give it a particular relevance for a particular group in a particular environment.

The possibilities are innumerable if this service is available. It may be left, however, to individual schools to deal with this as a group. Where a school has only one four-track recorder it may be asking too much to expect it to tie up the tape-recorder for almost the whole of every day. Perhaps such a school could be responsible for all the radio broadcasts on one day of the week; this might be easier to remember than who is doing which broadcast.

In this situation the making of duplicates might be more difficult than it would be in the teachers' centre, which would probably have considerably more equipment than most primary or middle schools. Enthusiasm and goodwill will undoubtedly solve this problem.

Storage of tapes

Each school will decide for itself whether the taped broadcasts will be classified on their own or included with other tapes. There seems no valid reason for segregating them, whether they are in reel-to-reel or cassette form.

The pamphlets issued by the broadcasting authorities are not standardized in size so their storage is a little more difficult than the storage of the reels or cassettes themselves. It is convenient for shelves for tapes to be more closely spaced than shelves for books, and this means that it will not be easy to file the notes for each series with the tapes. If the shelves are put further apart, the pamphlets will flop because they are taller than the tapes they accompany.

To leave the notes loose is almost certain to lead to their disappearance or, at best, to their disintegration. Either situation would be unfortunate because a good deal of excellent illustrative material is provided, which can be mounted and added to the illustrations collection. One way of protecting them is to put them inside pamphlet boxes where, although they are loose, they are controlled to a small extent (see Plate 8).

Ring binders are, on the whole, a satisfactory answer. When the tape is being processed for adding to the stock of the library, two labels will be prepared containing the call number with the bracketed accession number – one for sticking on the container and the other for the reel. If a third is made at the same time, this can be attached to the top right corner of the outside cover of the pamphlet. When holes have been punched through the pamphlet it can be inserted into its place in the classified sequence within the ring binder. The librarian should be generous with ring binders rather than have to cram the pamphlets.

Radiovision programmes will bring together a tape and a filmstrip (which may be cut up into slides) for each programme. These can be kept together in a box like those illustrated in Plate 4. If this combination is filed with the tape collection then all its items take the call number of 'TAPE' irrespective of the fact that one is a filmstrip or a slideset. This is done to keep them together.

The cardboard boxes in which some tapes are supplied tend to have rounded corners and edges rather than square ones, so that they do not stand easily on their sides without support. Philips make a plastic box, square-edged and able to stand on a shelf by itself; this is often preferred to their interlocking racks taking six boxes in each. Similar racks are available for cassettes, but in some the cassettes fit just too tightly so that, in extracting one, others are inclined to come too; the cassette container can be at fault. These containers, although light, can stand by themselves and be stored on a library shelf.

For those who feel that cassettes are too small for normal shelving there is a plastic insert, shown in Plate 9. This can be used in the drawer of a catalogue cabinet. One of the drawbacks of a group of cassettes is the drab appearance of their black spines, blank apart from the label with the call number. This tray separates the cassettes and allows the coloured part to be seen. Another possible way of making them more attractive might be to use a revolving stand of the kind shown in Plate 16, which is used in some record shops. This takes up to two hundred cassettes or other such items.

Plate 16 Revolving stand for tapes

Films, filmloops, reel-to-reel and cassette tapes, by the nature of their packaging, give a depressing effect when compared with attractive bookjackets; the librarian has to use his ingenuity to give them some appeal.

Miscellaneous

The types of media in the school library will vary; about a dozen of the most common have been discussed in this chapter. Another half dozen will perhaps be represented in twos and threes. On the whole they will be classified, catalogued and recorded in the subject index for the purposes of information retrieval.

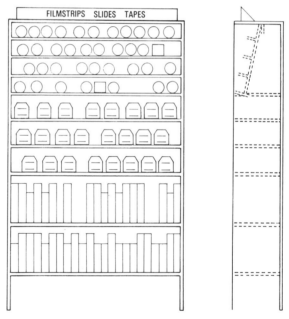

Fig. 28

Filmloops are small and *films* are not likely to be large because of their cost. As it will be convenient to keep certain media together these two can be accommodated within the provision already made. Figures 28, 29 and 30 show three possibilities. Where small items like filmloops have to be placed on normal shelving it may be necessary to place some kind of buffer behind them to prevent their constant slipping to the back.

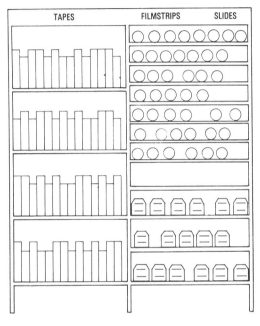

Fig. 29

Games are gradually appearing in greater quantities. Their boxes receive harsh treatment and, like many books, are better strengthened at the outset and their contents listed and pasted to the inside of the box for checking. The name of the game should appear in the subject index and the word 'GAME' inserted where the classification number would normally be. The dimensions of the boxes vary, so their storage is not so simple; but a place should be found, labelled and kept for them.

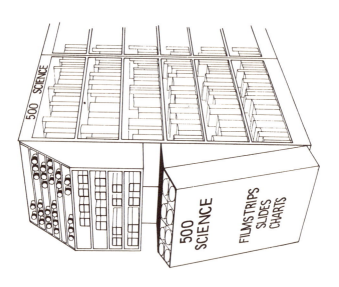

Fig. 30

(*a*)

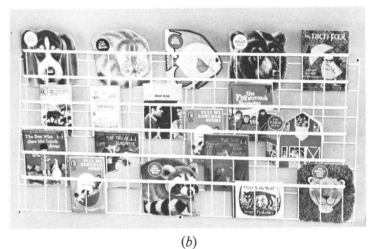

(*b*)

Plate 17   Display stands
   (a) Free standing (b) Wall fixture

Kits, too, can be awkward for shelving but as they have an information value they will be classified, catalogued and recorded in the subject index. Because they will be kept in classified order, a parallel sequence can probably be arranged at the end of the classification sequence. Alternatively they could be kept in the kind of display stand shown in Plate 17.

Transparencies, as has already been suggested, may not collect in the library but rather tend to remain with the teachers who make them. If there are any they can be classified, catalogued and recorded in the subject index. Where there is a record collection like the one shown in Plate 13 the transparencies might be kept there also. Or each could be inserted into a polythene pocket, all to be kept as a collection in a large pamphlet box.

In time *videotapes* may be added to the school's resources but it is possible that, for some time, they may be regarded as too costly to be safely kept readily accessible on the shelves of the library. However, with all the development that is already taking place, the day will come when the videotapes will be as accessible as the other media.

Addresses of suppliers mentioned in the text

ART METAL, Dominant House, 85 Queen Victoria Street, London EC4V 4HS. Telephone 01-236 5341.

G. BLUNT and SONS LTD, Gunners Way, Brockhurst, Gosport. Telephone Gosport 84541.

BRAINOS SLIDE LIBRARY, KOROSEAL TRADING COMPANY, 225 Southwark Bridge Road, London SE1 0DN. Telephone 01-407 4004.

DON GRESSWELL LTD, Bridge House, Grange Park, London N21 1RB. Telephone 01-360 6622/4.

JUNIOR BOOKS LTD, Earls Road, Grangemouth. Telephone Grangemouth 4533.

LIBRACO LTD, Lombard Wall, Charlton, London SE7. Telephone 01-858 3308.

RAILEX, FRANK WILSON (FILING) LTD, Railex House, 13 City Road, London EC1. Telephone 01-628 4507.

STOR CABINETS LTD, Furze Platt, Maidenhead, Berks. Telephone 0628-26216.

TERRAPIN RESKA LTD, Bond Avenue, Bletchley, Bucks. Telephone 090–82 4971.

A. WEST and SONS LTD, (Tubes for charts), 684 Mitcham Road, Croydon, Surrey. Telephone 01-688 6171.

DIANA WYLLIE LTD, 3 Park Road, Baker Street, London
NW1. Telephone 01-723 7333 and 3330.

Stationery and equipment for different types of strip indexing are
available under the trade names of specific suppliers, such as:

ART METAL – Stripindex
  Dominant House, 85 Queen Victoria Street, London EC4V
  4HS.
REMINGTON RAND – Linedex
  Division of Sperry Rand Ltd, 65 Holborn Viaduct, London
  EC1.
RONEO VICKERS – Stripdex
  Roneo House, Lansdowne Road, Croydon, Surrey, CR9
  2HA.

Periodicals as sources of information

Audio-Visual Aids. Published by the Educational Foundation for Visual Aids (EFVA). Since June 1971 a new series has been published consisting of a combined descriptive list of charts, films, filmstrips, records, slides, tapes, transparencies, etc. A list of distributors' names and addresses, a title index and a price list are included. The address is 33 Queen Anne Street, London W1M 0AL. Telephone 01-636 5742.

Visual Education. Published by the National Committee for Audio-Visual Aids in Education (NCAVAE). There are eleven issues per year; the August and September issues appear as one and the enlarged issue for July is a year-book with a directory of educational resources and a useful book-list. It is useful to subscribe to a scheme known as VENISS (Visual Educational National Information Service for Schools) which includes *Visual Education,* the year-book and the national catalogue of audio-visual aids. Enquiries should be sent to the address of EFVA given above.

The School Librarian. Published by the School Library Association, Premier House, 150 Southampton Row, London WC1B 5AR. Telephone 01-837 8114.

Treasure Chest for Teachers: Services Available to Teachers and Schools. Published by the Schoolmaster Publishing Company Ltd, Derbyshire House, St Chad's Street, London WC1H 8AJ. Telephone 01-837 6331.

Index

Numbers in italics denote illustrations